Montana Bed and Breakfast Guide and Cookbook

by Janet Ollila Colberg
with photos by Steve Colberg

Summer Kitchen Press
Helena, Montana

Library of Congress Cataloging-in-Publication Data
Colberg, Janet Ollila
Montana Bed and Breakfast Guide and Cookbook
Includes bibliographical references and index.
1. Bed and breakfast accommodations -- Montana -- Guidebooks.
2. Cookbooks. 3. Montana -- History. 4. West (U.S.) -- Description
and travel. I. Colberg, Janet Ollila. II. Colberg, Steve

TX907.3.M85 C65 2000   647.9478603 20
ISBN: 0-9653647-3-9

Published and distributed by Summer Kitchen Press
Cover, book design, typesetting by Summer Kitchen Press

For additional copies call 1-406-442-5237 or 1-800-418-5237, send
email to JColberg@BiggerSky.com or send $14.95 plus $2.00 shipping
and handling to Summer Kitchen Press, 314 Chaucer Street, Helena, MT
59601. Volume and wholesale discounts are available. The Summer
Kitchen Press World Wide Web site is http://www.BiggerSky.com/SKP

Second Edition

Manufactured in the United States

Montana Bed and Breakfast Guide and Cookbook

Contents

Charlie Russell Country 137

Yellowstone Country 179

Foreward by Governor Marc Racicot

OFFICE OF THE GOVERNOR
STATE OF MONTANA

MARC RACICOT
GOVERNOR

STATE CAPITOL
HELENA, MONTANA 59620-0801

FOREWARD

Welcome to the wonderful world of Montana hospitality. And welcome to the state explored and documented by the Lewis and Clark Expedition of 1804 - 1806. The beauty of Montana remains as breathtaking as Lewis and Clark found it.

But what makes Montana truly a treasure is, quite simply, its people. There aren't many of us -- only 856,000 by last official count -- scattered over 148,000 square miles of some of the most diverse and powerful landscape in the United States. But the people who are here treat each other with the respect, civility and regard you would expect from neighbors of yesteryear.

Travelers to Montana have come to know the quality of our bed and breakfast homes through the first edition of *Montana Bed and Breakfast Guide and Cookbook*. The new second edition features over one hundred homes and more delicious recipes that are unique to Montana.

I hope you enjoy yourself immensely and return. And I hope you come to believe, as I do, that Montana truly is what America was.

Sincerely,

MARC RACICOT
Governor

TELEPHONE: (406) 444-3111 FAX: (406) 444-5529

Dedication

In 1994, we dedicated the first edition of this book to "the keepers of the inn, who share their homes with travelers each day." Again, we dedicate this edition, *Montana Bed and Breakfast Guide and Cookbook, Second Edition*, to bed and breakfast hosts and hostesses.

We believe that God commissions each of us to actively care for one another. We personally appreciate the care we received from the innkeepers we met and interviewed while writing this book. God and these unique people are the inspiration to keep us going.

For example, a message from Hebrews in calligraphy encircles the perimeter of a dining room as a ceiling border and says, "Be Not Forgetful to Entertain Strangers, for Thereby Some Have Entertained Angels Unaware," Hebrews 13:2.

Another message, a rubbing also in calligraphy, was sent to us and says, "Christ is the Head of This House. The Unseen Guest at every Meal. The Silent Listener to every Conversation."

Another message on a sampler, "Wrought by Mary Sedgwick, 1836, Dublin, Ireland, 13 years old," says, "Be Virtuous If You Would Be Happy."

This is but a sampling of the sayings and stories on the ensuing pages. We hope you enjoy using this book as much as we and the bed and breakfast hosts and hostesses have enjoyed preparing it for you.

Acknowledgments

We thank our family and friends for the support and encouragement they give us. The people who gave hours of time and talent making this book a reality deserve acknowledgment.

We especially appreciate the editing capability of our daughter-in-law, **Laura Christensen Colberg.** Her skill and attention to detail makes this book more enjoyable to you as a reader.

The support and encouragement of our friend **Karen Enhelder** was important when traveling those muddy miles to the far reaches of Montana in early springtime.

It was fortunate to have the help of **Bonnie Meyer** who supervised an entire cadre of cooks so we could have the recipes kitchen-tested. Beside Bonnie there are seven other tasters and testers. They are **Angela** and **Solomon Meyer**, **Sue** and **Mackenzie Struble**, **Mariana Mink, Daunya Peterson** and **Charlotte Stouder**.

Two other people have been a boon to the bed and breakfast industry in Montana and deserve recognition. **Marge Anderson** is a good friend and former owner of the Chalet in Great Falls. Many comfortable hours were spent enjoying Marge's personality and hospitality.

Dale McAfee hosts the Columns in White Sulphur Springs. Besides operating his bed and breakfast home, Dale contributes time and enthusiasm to the Castle Museum of White Sulphur Springs making it standout among our Montana museums.

We thank **Robert Clark** and the Montana Historical Society and the Helena Lewis and Clark Reference Library for the excellent access to resources materials. It is a joy to work with all of you.

Introduction

The tradition of a traveler's "homestay" originated in Europe. A traveler arriving at a train station or a bus terminal weary and hungry could inquire about a place to stay. Homes near the station had a room or two to share. Depots kept the names of these homes where, for a modest fee, visitors were welcomed to bed and breakfast as part of the family.

In recent years, this tradition has come to the United States. Visiting bed and breakfast homes is a delightful way to relax, to meet people and to enjoy the diverse cultures of America. Montana is no exception to this travel phenomenon.

Travel Montana, the tourism agency of the State of Montana, uses six regional names to describe the state. To avoid confusion, *Montana Bed and Breakfast Guide and Cookbook, Second Edition,* uses the same designation. First, we highlight the treasures of Montana in Gold West Country. Next, we move to Glacier Country and the famous Glacier National Park. Third, in Russell Country, we celebrate Montana's favorite yarn spinner and artist, Charlie Russell. We move to Yellowstone Country named for Yellowstone Park, declared a National Monument in 1872. Next, we move to Custer Country and more of Montana's engaging history. Last, but not least, Missouri River Country is for the river explored and charted by the Lewis and Clark Expedition.

This book features a variety of bed and breakfast homes and a cookbook of their favorite recipes. Collecting information was done by on-site visits and host interviews to each of the bed and breakfast homes and their owners. In two instances, a representative was present rather than the owner. In all instances, the hosts live on or next to the premises of the bed and breakfast home. They have personal joy and investment in the hospitality they offer. All offer a full breakfast. In addition, nearly all have one or more rooms with a private bath. Contact numbers are provided so travelers can inquire about suitable rooms and rates.

Each section of *Montana Bed and Breakfast Guide and Cookbook, Second Edition*, provides a regional map along with descriptions and pictures of each home within the region. Because history and heritage are fascinating to many travelers, historical details and unique ideas are included. The description of each home includes details about the setting, a physical description of the home, host family preferences and ideas and addresses and contact numbers for further information. Many homes have contributed one or more favorite recipes.

Some homes featured in *Montana Bed and Breakfast Guide and Cookbook* are on the beautiful backroads and byways of rural Montana. The scarcity of food services prompts owners to serve an evening meal or to establish a restaurant. Included in *Montana Bed and Breakfast Guide and Cookbook* are recipes for all meals of the day and dishes that are novel to Montana. For instance, your mouth will water at the thought of Aspen Plank Trout. You will delight at the fluffiness of Sylvia Shaw's Baking Powder Biscuits, or at the ease of preparing your own Paradise Strawberry Pie.

Noteworthy to this second edition is detail about the Lewis and Clark Expedition as it applies to individual bed and breakfast homes. In the years 2004-2006, Montana celebrates the bicentennial of the journey of the explorers. Meriweather Lewis received this commission:

20 June 1803

The object of your mission is to explore the Missouri River and such principal stream of it, as, by its course and communication with the waters of the Pacific Ocean . . . may offer the most direct and practicable water communication across this continent for the purposes of commerce.

Thomas Jefferson to Meriweather Lewis

Meriweather Lewis asked for the appointment of Captain William Clark to the expedition. Bernard DeVoto, in his famous chronology of the Lewis and Clark adventures has this to say: "the two (Lewis and Clark) agreed and worked together with a mutuality unknown elsewhere in the history of exploration and rare in any kind of human association."

The other thirty-two persons on the expedition were invaluable to its success. However, the third person who deserves special recognition is Sacagawea, daughter of the Tendoy Shoshone and young hostage of the Minnetarees. Sacagawea's name is noted as part of Lewis' observations when the expedition settled in Mandan for the winter of 1804. In Mandan, the expedition hired Touissant Charbonneau, a French fur trader and interpreter of the Minnetaree language. Sacagawea was one of Charbonneau's Indian wives. Her strongest appearance is at an accidental reconnection with her brother of the Tendoy Shoshone at Horse Prairie. Gaining the trust of her brother, she is able to help Lewis get horses for traversing the rugged mountains, called the Rocky Mountains, that divide the headwaters of the Missouri and Columbia Rivers.

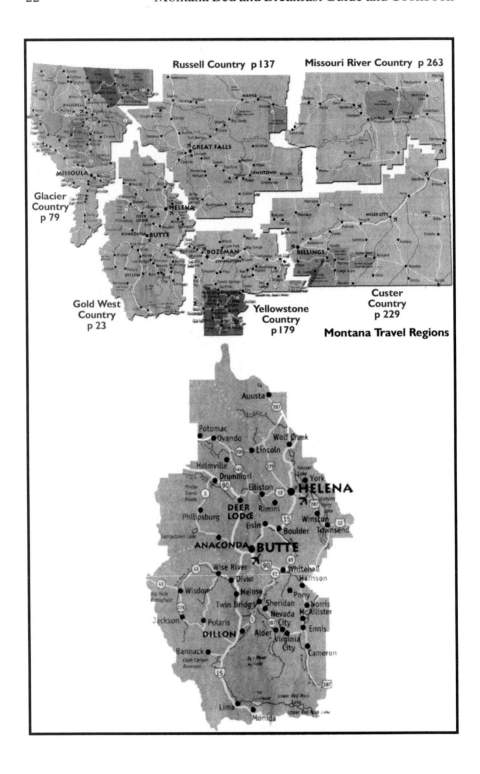

Russell Country p 137

Missouri River Country p 263

Glacier Country p 79

Gold West Country p 23

Yellowstone Country p 179

Custer Country p 229

Montana Travel Regions

Gold West Country

If bricks and mortar could talk and old oak pocket doors could open on a scene from yesteryear, there would be grand stories to tell. Our adventure begins in Gold West Country, named for the Gold Rush Era that gave Montana its biggest population boom. Adventurers and entrepreneurs, cattlemen and pioneers found their way West. Taking those same trails, you will visit places like Alder Gulch and Bannack where ancestral history begins for many bed and breakfast owners.

You will meet Jean Cooney Roberts whose great-grandfather was a gold prospector. He followed the gold rush from Virginia City and Bannack to Diamond City in the Big Belt Mountains above White Sulphur Springs. You will meet Connie and Diana who have industriously restored the Collins Mansion in Great Falls. This project celebrates the life and times of T. E. and Lavinia Collins. Drawn by the gold strike in the Castle Mountains, T. E. Collins originally settled in White Sulphur Springs. He later moved to Great Falls where he was a banker and businessman.

The freighters and stagecoach bosses were important to Montana's settlement. People like Rita and Joe Christiaens bring history to life. Rita's great-grandmother came to the Dupuyer area on a freighter like the one portrayed in Charlie Russell's painting, *Jerkline*. In *Jerkline*, the drays are loaded with goods and supplies for the pioneer settlements and mining camps. Stoneheart Inn, restored by Judith and Michael Tholt, is an example of a stagecoach inn of yesteryear. The Blackfoot Inn of Howard and Peggy Fly is a restored mercantile where mule trains met the freighters to disperse goods to Swan Valley homesteads.

The folks featured in the *Montana Bed and Breakfast Guide and Cookbook, Second Edition*, are extraordinary citizens of Montana. They are preservationists commemorating many historical aspects of a magnificent state. Our travels begin in Dillon with a stay at the Centennial Inn and Restaurant with the James Family.

Horse Prairie

People in southwestern Montana are proud of their history. Beaverhead County has strong ties to the Lewis and Clark Expedition of the early 1800's. Meriweather Lewis and William Clark, commissioned by President Thomas Jefferson, explored, mapped and documented the area covered by the Louisiana Purchase of 1803. Lewis and Clark were practical scouts and named places for what they saw. Horse Prairie received its name for the horses of Tendoy and it remains a part of Beaverhead County.

Sacagawea, a young Indian woman important to the Lewis and Clark Expedition, came from the Tendoy Shoshone tribe. As a girl, Sacagawea was captured and held hostage by the Minnetarees. Lewis and Clark met Sacagawea in the Mandan villages in Dakota. She was married to guide Touissant Charbonneau, whose scouting and interpreting skills were valuable to the expedition. Sacagawea's role as an interpreter and as a symbol of nurture catch a reader's attention in the journals about the Lewis and Clark Expedition.

Lewis, Sacagawea and other members of the expedition went to the Shoshone in search of horses. At Horse Prairie, Sacagawea unexpectedly met her brother, a leader of the Tendoy. With this auspicious turn of events, Lewis and Sacagawea procured horses for crossing the rugged terrain of the continental divide between the Missouri and Columbia River Basins.

Centennial Inn

About a half-century after Lewis and Clark's exploration of the Beaverhead, the Gold Rush of 1863 brought prospectors and settlers to Bannack in the Beaverhead Valley and to Virginia City. Early historical accounts of people like the James Family rekindle a curiosity about the scouts and pioneers of

Beaverhead County. The Jameses have a ranch on Horse Prairie. They also own **Centennial Inn Bed and Breakfast and Restaurant** in Dillon. Their ancestors were enticed to Virginia City and the area around Bannack by the promise of gold. Jeannie James' great-father, D. W. Tilton, saw the hunger of Montanans for reading materials. Tilton brought the first printing press to Montana and was instrumental in establishing the *Montana Post*, Virginia City's first newspaper. In 1865, with Thomas Dimsdale, he printed the first book published in Montana, Dimsdale's *Vigilantes*.

At the Centennial Inn and Restaurant, Jeannie James' guestrooms and the main floor restaurant are meticulously clean. The rooms have luxurious linens, hand-embroidered ecru bed covers and Victorian jacquard lace curtains. Beside a queen bed or two, each room has a highboy or armoire, antique chairs and a marble-topped stand or library table. Many items are heirlooms or antique replicas. A piano lamp, circa 1870, is an antique from

the Gold Rush Era in Virginia City. The rooms have eclectic ceiling lamps, collected, refurbished and installed by Sandy James. Ancestral histories and art by Jeannie James and Mary Tilton personalize the guestrooms. Rooms named for the family honor the Tiltons,

Gendalls, Brenners and Jameses.

Beside cattle ranching, Horse Prairie Ranch has an aspenwood sawmill. The light hues of aspen make it well-suited for furniture. The following recipe for trout called Aspen Plank Trout is served on an aspen plank hewn at the lumber mill. The Centennial Restaurant is a family project. Owen James perfected the Beer Batter Pancakes that are requested for breakfast. Sandy creates house dressing called Red Blue Cheese Dressing and Amy James is the restaurant hostess. The dressing recipe is for a large batch; it may be decreased proportionally for household use.

Centennial Aspen Plank Trout

small aspen plank of various sizes
trout from Montana trout farms
or
fresh stream trout, cleaned
½ cup flour
½ teaspoon salt
2 tablespoons vegetable oil
2 tablespoons butter

Select an aspen plank and soak it in cold water for 3 hours. The length of the plank is to be the same length as the trout. Combine flour and salt in plastic bag and coat fish thoroughly with flour mixture. Melt butter and add oil; heat. Sauté fish on its side in hot oil mixture until golden brown. BROWN ON ONE SIDE ONLY. Flip fish so that sautéed side is on aspen plank. Bake in oven at 400°F until topside of trout is golden brown. Fish should be flaky and cooked through. Note that the quaking aspen flavor permeates the trout. Serve trout on the plank. Put plank on bamboo place mat. Lavishly garnish with fresh fruit and vegetables.

Sandy's Red Blue Cheese Dressing

1¾ cups ketchup
1¼ cups vegetable oil (do not use olive oil)
1¼ cups honey
1½ tablespoons vinegar
1 tablespoon Worcestershire
sauce
½ teaspoon onion powder
½ teaspoon garlic powder
½ teaspoon salt
½ teaspoon dry mustard
½ teaspoon ground pepper
1½ cups crumbled blue cheese

Combine first 10 ingredients and blend by hand with a wire whisk. DO NOT blend in food processor. Add blue cheese crumbles. Use covered glass container for refrigerator storage.

Host and Hostess: Sandy and Jeannie James

Address and Contact Numbers:
125 South Washington, Dillon, MT 59725
1-406-683-4454

The Inn at Pioneer Mountain Farm

Tucked away in the rolling hills of Beaverhead Valley is the **Inn at Pioneer Mountain Farm Bed and Breakfast**. The hostess, Ann Dooling, says,

"As I drive down this lane of cottonwoods, I forget that the rest of the world exists." It is a blessed environment where newborn goat kids frolic, jumping at the pure joy of being alive.

Tom and Ann Dooling broaden the experience of their guests as

they share the excitement of world travel to places such as China, Italy and South America. They produce cashmere, which is the product of processed goat down. The Doolings oversee their cottage industry from the raising and shearing of the goats to the completed knits which are shipped all over the world. Six electric looms are in daily operation. Ann creates the intricate patterns and trains each person who handles a loom. Her main creations are soft knits for infants, toddlers and children.

In addition to managing a cashmere business, Tom Dooling restores buildings. The Pioneer Inn was once the Diamond Bar Inn. It fell into disrepair and was moved by the Doolings and resurrected as a guest home with

five bedrooms. The bedrooms
retain the warm knotty pine pan-
eling and old room numbers of
the Diamond Bar Inn. They have
shared and private baths and
luxurious king beds.

Host and Hostess: Tom and Ann Dooling

Address and Contact Numbers:
3299 Anderson Lane, Dillon, MT
59725
1-888-683-5445
www.innatpoineermtn.com
e-mail: ann@montanaknits.com

Blue Heron

Gold West Country twinkles in the early morning sunlight. The trill of a meadowlark breaks over the valley. While hiking a woodland trail you might see a cluster of lady's slipper orchids rising from the remains of a lightning-felled tree, or exclaim over the brilliance of a sapphire mined at Gem Mountain near Philipsburg.

Philipsburg is a peaceful little town on Pintlar Scenic Route One. Gem Mountain with its quality sapphire mines, and Rock Creek with its blue-ribbon trout fishing are just miles down the highway. In winter, our host reports that Discovery Basin ski hill is "delightful, personal and never crowded." And the chocolate chip cookies at the Discovery lunch counter are ready at ten, just after a couple of runs down the ski slope.

John Ohrmann and Myrlin Rasmussen own the **Blue Heron Bed and Breakfast** home in Philipsburg. Their mascot, the heron, inhabits every country of the world. A rookery of heron and the presence of other birds and wildlife are an added attraction for birders and naturalists.

Comforts of home are basic to a stay at the Blue Heron. It has one room with a private bath. The other five rooms share two full bathrooms. Fluffy white linens, large, comfy beds, spotless cleanliness and the smell of chocolate cheesecake baking in the oven complete the home's inviting atmosphere.

But there is more. Philipsburg is reputed to have 350 days when the sun shines. On those many clear days you can see the valley from your second story breakfast room. John

Ohrmann and his father Bill are established artists in the state of Montana. The bed and break-fast is frequently an artist's work sanctuary. Myrlin has an eye for detail that complements the art displayed at the Blue Heron.

And the cottage cobbler is a work of edible art with fresh fruits.

Cottage Cobbler

1½ cups flour
2 teaspoons baking powder
¼ teaspoon salt
$^1/_3$ cup sugar
1 egg
½ cup warm milk
½ cup melted butter
2 cups fruit or berries
1 egg, beaten
1 tablespoon dry tapioca
¾ cup sugar

Sift flour, baking powder, salt and sugar. Mix egg, tapioca, milk and butter. Combine egg and sugar mixtures until consistency of pudding. Spread fruit mixture over bottom of 9-inch round casserole. Spread pudding mixture over fruit. Bake at 350°F for 30 minutes. Top with whipped cream or ice cream. Serves 6-8.

Host and Hostess: John Ohrmann and Myrlin Rasmussen
Address and Contact Numbers:
138 West Broadway, Philipsburg, MT 59858
1-406-859-3856
www.blueheronmt.com
e-mail: blueheron@yahoo.com

Coleman-Fee Mansion

William Coleman was a successful miner who struck gold at Grasshopper Creek in Bannack. Coleman used his profits to settle in Deer Lodge and establish the town's first mercantile, Coleman and Company. Presently,

Betty and Ronda Stiehl, a mother-daughter team, operate the **Coleman-Fee Mansion Bed and Breakfast**. They purchased the mansion in 1996 and honor the two owners who contributed to the commercial life of Deer Lodge.

The Coleman-Fee Mansion is perfect in every way. Old diaries say Coleman built the 1890's mansion so his family could enjoy the good life. Coleman spared no expense to see that the best workmanship and materials were used to construct one of the most impressive homes in Gold West Country. William Coleman did not live to see the difficult times his family faced. He died in 1924 and the family lost their fortune in the stock market crash of 1927.

A balance within this Queen Anne-style Victorian mansion is ornate enough to be interesting, yet simple enough to be unpretentious. Massive golden oak panels in the foyer, living room and sitting room came from Minnesota. Throughout the home, period wallpaper has been painstakingly preserved. Thirteen original stained-glass windows and several panels of bronze-encased crystal panes of waterglass grace the main rooms. A distinctive rosewood fireplace with Belgian tile is part of the largest guest bedroom.

The Stiehls have refurbished details of the home that make guests comfortable. There

are private baths in all but one of the four second-story bedrooms. All have either queen or king beds except the Teddy Room with twin beds for young guests. A suite of rooms on the first floor is equipped with computers and fax lines for executive stays. It has its own enclosed porch and entry.

The Coleman-Fee is not only a bed and breakfast get-away, its environs are beautiful for wedding receptions, birthday parties and other events catered by the Stiehls. Betty and Ronda use the following recipes for entertaining.

Breakfast Quiche

1 9-inch pie crust
8 eggs
½ cup black olives
½ cup chopped ham
½ cup chopped fried bacon
¼ cup chopped green peppers
¼ cup chopped green onions
1¼ cup grated cheddar cheese
¾ cup sweet cream or
¾ cup milk with 1 teaspoon sugar
2 tablespoons Mrs. Dash
1 tablespoon fresh parsley or
1 teaspoon dried parsley

Beat eggs, add sweet cream, set aside. Mix black olives, ham, bacon, green peppers, green onions, Mrs. Dash, parsley and cheddar cheese. Place in unbaked piecrust. Cover with egg mixture. Bake at 350°F for 45 minutes or until knife inserted in center comes out clean. Cool for 20 minutes, cut and serve.

Hot Chicken Salad

8 chicken breasts
2 cans mushroom soup
1 bunch scallions
1 cup chopped celery
1 can drained water chestnuts
1 cup Miracle Whip
3 cups oriental noodles

Cube chicken, barely cover with boiling water and cook until tender. To cooked chicken, add mushroom soup, scallions, celery, water chestnuts and Miracle Whip. Simmer for 15 minutes. Spoon mixture over a nest of oriental noodles and serve.

Hostesses: Ronda and Betty Stiehl
Address and Contact Numbers:
500 Missouri Avenue, Deer Lodge, MT 59722
1-888-888-2507, 1-406-846-2922

Blackfoot Inn

Until recently, Ovando was the little Montana town that time forgot. Today, Ovando's new bed and breakfast home, the **Blackfoot Inn and**

Commercial Company, is the hub of an active town. The owners of the Blackfoot are a delightful couple named Howard and Peggy Fly. They are enthusiastic preservationists. The objective of their history lesson is making Ovando come alive by honoring the pioneers of the valley. A pictorial and heritage guide is part of Ovando's museum.

Another history and geography lesson shows that on July 6, 1806, Lewis traversed the "Prairie of the Knobs" near Ovando. Centuries before, in the land formation of Montana, glacial changes brought melting and freezing action. Dirt in the wake of the glacier became large mounds that Lewis called "knobs covered with grass."

The site of the commercial company is not new. It began as a freighter station. The freighters hauled supplies from the Northern Pacific stop in Drummond to Ovando. A string of mules or packhorses would further distribute supplies to homesteads in the Swan River Valley. Today the remodeled Inn and Commercial Company serve mercantile and social interests in ways similar to the freighter station of yesteryear.

The rooms at the Blackfoot Inn are new. They all have private baths; their names honor early settlers. Harry Morgan, Ovando Valley's first game warden, is remembered for his kind heart. As the Robin Hood of Ovando Forest, Harry used confiscated poacher deer to provide meat for needy fami-

lies. There are rooms named for
Charley and Betsy Young.
Charley came to the valley as a
boy and grew into a man with a
reputation for honesty. His skill
as a trapper and furrier made his
beaver pelts coveted as far away
as Chicago. Betsy Young, his
sister, was the first white girl
born in the Ovando Valley.

In addition to the guestrooms, Peggy Fly has a commercial kitchen and Pear
Pie to share.

Pear Pie

Pie crust for 5 9-inch pie shells:
5 cups flour
2 teaspoons salt
1 teaspoon baking powder
2 cups shortening
1 egg
3 tablespoons vinegar
water

Sift flour, salt and baking powder. Add lard and mix with dry
ingredients until crumbly. Break
egg into a 1 cup-sized measuring cup. Add vinegar and fill to
the top with cold water. Mix and
add to the flour mixture. Divide into five pieces. Roll shells as needed for
pie.

Filling for 1 pie:
5 fresh pie pears, peeled and quartered or
1 30-ounce can pears, drained and quartered
¾ cup sugar
1/8 teaspoon salt
1 tablespoon cornstarch
1 teaspoon lemon rind
1 tablespoon lemon juice
½ teaspoon cinnamon
½ teaspoon ginger
¼ teaspoon mace
½ cup flour
¼ cup butter
1 pie shell

Line pie pan with pastry and fill with pears. Combine salt, cornstarch, lemon rind and ¼ cup of the sugar. Spread over pears. Combine remaining ingredients and crumble over top of pears and sugar mixture. Bake at 350°F for 45 minutes or until brown and bubbly.

Host and Hostess: Howard and Peggy Fly
Address and Contact Numbers:
Box 89, Ovando, MT 59854
1-406-793-5555
e-mail: blackfootinn@montana.com

Blackfoot Steamer

Before leaving Ovando, your stay would not be complete without a stop at the Blackfoot Steamer and Custom Ranch Design. Vickie and Ben Harbour have an espresso shop and craft items. Ben does custom design ironworks and makes the furniture and gift items sold in the store.

Shepherd's Pie

1½ pounds ground beef, drain
1 medium onion, chopped
1½ ounce can cut green beans
10¼ ounce can condensed tomato soup
6-8 potatoes
½ cup milk
¼ cup butter or margarine
½ teaspoon salt
¼ teaspoon pepper

In skillet, brown the meat and onions; season with salt and pepper. Add drained beans and tomato soup. Pour into 1½-quart casserole dish. Peel, cook, and mash the potatoes. Add milk and butter. Salt to taste. Top meat with mounds of potatoes and sprinkle with pepper. Bake at 350°F for 45 minutes. Serves 4-6.

Host and Hostess: Ben and Vickie Harbour
Address and Contact Numbers:
Blackfoot Steamer, Ovando, MT 59854
1-406-793-5527

Lumberjack Inn Bed and Breakfast

The **Lumberjack Inn Bed and Breakfast** is a log oasis carved out of the timberland surrounding Lincoln, Montana. Brent and Carla Anderson own and operate Conifer Logging Incorporated and the Lumberjack. They built the photogenic log home to share with families. A young guest enjoys the Lumberjack and says, "Dad, I want to go to that place where they have pears in jars with no labels."

Yes, a bit of old-fashioned Montana is alive and well at the Lumberjack. Not only is Carla a baker and homemaker, she collects antiques and salvages ancient washing machines, horse harnesses, wooden vessels and old fruit jars with zinc covers, and turns them into functional items such as planters and lamp fixtures. She savors old cookbooks and old pictures. A photographic history of the timber industry is framed and displayed at the Lumberjack.

Carla enjoys quotes from favorite Montanans. For guestrooms, she has framed quotes from Mike Mansfield, Montana's former ambassador to Japan, and from Norma Ashby, Montana's quintessential talk show host. And from John Steinbeck's *Travels With Charley* as Steinbeck told Charley, "I'm in love with Montana."

The guestroom details include log beds with quilted coverlets, oak-framed windows that look out over the wilderness, and a private bathroom stocked with fluffy towels and toiletries.

Fruit Pizza

Crust:
1/3 cup butter or margarine
1/3 cups sugar
2 eggs
1 teaspoon vanilla
3½ cups flour
2½ teaspoons baking powder
½ teaspoon salt
4 teaspoons milk

Bottom Filling:
4 ounces Philadelphia cream cheese
6 ounces prepared Cool Whip or whipped cream

Top Filling:
1 package strawberry junket or Danish dessert
2 cups cold water
½ cup sugar
3-ounce package strawberry Jell-O
5 cups sliced fruit in season

To make crust, blend butter and sugar until smooth. Add eggs, one at a time. Add vanilla and beat well. Sift flour, sugar, baking powder and salt together. Add 1/3 of flour to butter-sugar mixture, blend well and add a little

milk. Repeat process until all ingredients are mixed. Dust rolling pin and board with flour and roll dough to cover a 12-inch round pizza pan or pottery pie dish. Bake at 350°F about 10 minutes or until golden brown. Cool.

In a small bowl fold cream cheese and Cool Whip until blended. Spread on cooled cookie crust. Slice fresh fruits such as kiwi, pears, bananas, strawberries, apples, huckleberries, blueberries, raspberries or peaches

and arrange in spirals.

Follow directions for a Jell-O strawberry glaze or use the filling for Paradise Strawberry Pie (shown above) which is from Johnstad's Bed and Breakfast. Drizzle over spiraled fruit. Cut in wedges like pizza and serve. Serves 6-10.

Host and Hostess:
Brent and Carla Anderson
Address and Contact Numbers:
Highway 200 West, Lincoln, MT 59639
1-406-362-4815

The Bungalow

The **Bungalow Bed and Breakfast** has a nostalgia that tugs at the heartstrings of anyone who loves Montana. It contains memorabilia reminiscent of people who came and went in Montana's early, uproarious 1900's. First, it has the hand-

print of the architect, Robert C. Reamer, who built Yellowstone's Old Faithful Inn. He studied the lay of the land and envisioned the beauty of the Bungalow as it stands today. If you know where to look, you will see Charley Russell's derby still hanging on the hat rack. Signed Remington and Russell

prints turn up like ghosts in many corners of the Bungalow.

In these times, Helena's Cowboy Poet, Mike Logan, tips his hat back to let the splendor of the wilderness inspire new rhyme and rhythm. Listen closely and you hear his soft and mighty voice reciting a few verses to the wind. Monte Dolack, an artist of stature and whimsy, comes to the Bungalow for relaxation and renewal.

Hostess Pat O'Connell Anderson grew up at the Bungalow. She entertains

often, and her smiling blue eyes let you know she enjoys people. Guests naturally become friends. Pat is on Highway 287 four miles into the wilderness beyond Wolf Creek. Her food is delicious. Incidentally, the Bungalow is only twenty miles from the Missouri River's famed Gates of the

Mountains. Lewis and Clark named it for the optical illusion of mountains holding back a river and then moving, letting your boat continue down the river.

Bungalow Pasta Salad

1 package multicolored rotini pasta, cooked and cooled
½ cup chopped sweet or red onion
½ cup chopped celery
1 cup small broccoli flowerettes
1 cup thinly sliced zucchini
1 small can sliced black olives
chopped sun-dried tomatoes to taste
1½ cups garlic/cheese Italian dressing
¼ cup chopped fresh basil

Combine all ingredients except basil. Marinate overnight in refrigerator. Stir in basil when ready to serve.

Grilled Lime Chicken

6-8 chicken breasts, halved, boneless, skinned
juice of 10 limes
8 large cloves of garlic, sliced

Marinate chicken in lime and garlic mixture in Zip-Loc bag for 30-60 minutes. Grill until juices run clear, about 15 -20 minutes. Serve with mango-lime salsa or drizzle with honey butter.

Mango-Lime Salsa

1 mango, finely chopped
½ cup red onion, chopped
juice of 1 lime
2 tablespoons balsamic vinegar
2 tablespoons olive oil
Combine ingredients and serve with chicken.

Hostess: Pat O'Connell Anderson
Address and Contact Numbers:
2020 Highway 287, Wolf Creek, MT 59648
1-888-286-4250, 1-406-235-4276
e-mail: bngalow@aol.com
Location:
Near Wolf Creek, take exit 228 from Highway 15
to Highway 287. Go 1.2 miles northwest on
Highway 287. Turn left, open gate and go .8
miles on dirt road to Bungalow.

Sanders of Helena

The saga of Gold West Country becomes more refined as you explore Helena, the capital city of Montana. The number of mansions in Helena is proportional to the riches that flowed from the Last Chance gold strike of 1864. Four Georgians in search of colors (gold) gave the gulch one last "look-see;" the rest is history. With the exception of the copper kings,

every entrepreneur in Montana Territory seems to have built an edifice in Helena to proclaim a personal wealth generated by the Last Chance gold strike.

The **Sanders of Helena Bed and Breakfast** commemorates the life of Harriet and Wilbur Fisk Sanders. W. F. Sanders was the nephew of Territorial Governor Sidney Edgerton. Sanders first surfaced as a self-appointed champion of the people and a member of the Vigilantes of Virginia City. His first house on Idaho Street in Virginia City still stands. After the hanging of the Plummer gang by the Vigilantes, it is said that Virginia City had such an honest citizenry you "could leave a pouch of gold nuggets in the street, unguarded, and it would still be there the next morning."

W. F. Sanders moved to Helena as a barrister. He was a born leader. Sanders begin a civic effort that culminated in establishing the Montana Historical Society. Harriet, trained as a school-teacher, was a leader, too. She promoted a woman's right to a free public education. Her support of a woman's right to vote was acknowledged by a personal letter from fellow suffragette, Susan B. An-

thony, dated October 2, 1895. The Sanders Bed and Breakfast has a copy of the letter. It would be a quarter of a century after 1895 that American women gained the right to vote. Enactment of Article Nineteen of the Constitution of the United States occurred on August 26, 1920.

Bobbi Uecker and Rock Ringling have owned this premier bed and breakfast home for thirteen years. Two young sons have changed Bobbi and Rock's schedule, but the dedication to fine lodging, dining and assisting guests remains the same. The location of the Sanders makes it easy for business people to work, whether their destination is the Capitol Complex or Downtown Helena. The central location also makes walking to key places possible. The Myrna Loy Center for the Performing Arts, the Original Governor's Mansion, Grandstreet Theater, the Cathedral of St. Helena and the Holter Museum are but a few nearby attractions.

The Sanders is a stately Queen Anne-style Victorian home. Eighty percent of the furnishings are original to the mansion. A particular room-sized shower with two showerheads for you and your significant other will make you smile; there is no need for a shower curtain. Accompanying this novelty is a bridal bed veiled in Scandinavian nuptial tulle. The Ringling Circus is part of Rock's heritage. A signature piece of

memorabilia crowned the forehead of the lead elephant in one of the three-ring circus acts.

The *Montana Cookbook* featured this original recipe from the Sanders.

French Toast With Sautéed Fruit

4 eggs
1 cup milk
2 tablespoons sugar
juice of one orange
juice of ½ lime
1½ teaspoons vanilla
8 ½ -inch slices of French bread

Fruit Topping:
1 cup sliced strawberries
1 cup sliced apples
1 cup orange slices
1 cup raspberry jam
3 tablespoons butter
1 teaspoon nutmeg
4 tablespoons triple sec

Combine milk, sugar, juices and vanilla. Set mixture aside. Melt butter and sauté fruit. Add raspberry jam, triple sec and nutmeg to fruit. Reduce heat and gently and occasionally stir until fruit is hot. Dip slices of bread in egg mixture, coating both sides thoroughly. Cook on griddle or in skillet over medium heat until both sides are brown, turning just once. Place French toast on serving plates and glaze with ¾ cup sautéed fruit. Sprinkle with powdered sugar. Serves 8.

Host and Hostess: Bobbi Uecker and Rock Ringling
Address and Contact Numbers:
328 North Ewing Street, Helena, MT 59601
1-406-442-3309
www.sandersbb.com

Barrister

A kaleidoscope of color from antique waterglass adds brightness to the elegant **Barrister Bed and Breakfast** owned by Nick Jacques. The history of the Barrister represents a settled time of pioneer life in Helena. Herman Gens had the home built in 1874. He had no direct connection to the Gold Rush. Gens and his Jewish compatriots had connections to merchants in New York. He worked

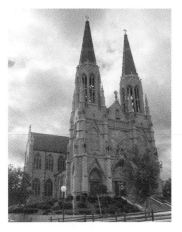

hard to honor the refined tastes of the frontier's wealthy families.

Because of its proximity to St. Helena Cathedral, the Barrister was formerly a rectory for Catholic priests. In 1975, Gary Duff, a specialist in computer-assisted architectural design, began an extensive restoration of the home and added skylights to intensify its beauty. A particular upstairs window frames a unique view of the Sleeping Giant in the distance with the spires of St. Helena Cathedral in the foreground.

Nick Jacques continues to add elegant details to the Barrister. Particularly fetching is an antique Singer sewing machine cabinet, which holds a small sink. With a twinkle in his eye, Nick quips, "I just tell guests to pump the foot treadle vigorously to get water."

The Barrister hosts a hospitality hour daily at five-thirty. It gives Nick and his staff time to entertain their guests in the parlour and tell them about the amenities of the Barrister and the sites to see within walking or driving distance of the mansion. Groups who gather for Christmas parties, weddings and business meetings find the home, with its 2000 square feet of common area, adequate to meet their needs. Stuffed Apple-Brandy French Toast from the *Best of Friends, Too* by Darlene Glantz Skees remains a breakfast favorite.

Stuffed Apple-Brandy French Toast

1 loaf day-old French bread
12 eggs
2 cups 2% milk
½ cup brandy
1 tablespoon vanilla
2 8-ounce packages softened cream cheese
4 sliced Granny Smith apples
4 tablespoons sugar

Topping:
½ cup sugar
2 teaspoons cinnamon
1/8 teaspoon nutmeg

Combine the topping ingredients and set aside. Slice French bread into 1-inch slices and arrange to cover a 9x13-inch pan coated with vegetable spray. Spread cream cheese over bread and a layer of apples; add ½ of the topping over the apples. Add a second layer of bread and apples. Mix eggs, milk, brandy, vanilla and sugar. Beat lightly and pour over bread. Spread with remaining topping. Bake at 400°F for 30 minutes. Serve with cinnamon syrup.

Cinnamon Syrup

1 cup white corn syrup
1 cup sugar
¼ cup water
½ teaspoon ground cinnamon
½ cup evaporated milk

Mix all ingredients except evaporated milk in saucepan and bring to boil. Boil 2 minutes. Let cool for 5 minutes and add evaporated milk. Serve warm.

Host: Nick Jacques
Address and Contact Numbers:
416 North Ewing Street, Helena, MT 59601
1-406-443-7330

Appleton Inn

The **Appleton Inn Bed and Breakfast** is a turn-of-the-century Victorian-style Painted Lady. The colors chosen by Tom and Cheryl to represent the Appleton are cream with accents of apple green and deep rose. Its name honors planner and designer, George S. Appleton.

The eye-catching design of the wrap-around porch breaks the steep line of the gambrel roof.

Attention to design continues as you walk through spindled cherrywood arches that separate the foyer and the two parlors. Family heirlooms and art objects exhibit a Victorian theme upstairs and down. Tom operates the Appleton Heirloom Furniture Company and uses his knowledge about antiques for authentic restoration and furniture building.

The Appleton has six rooms with private baths. A favorite with the children is the Family Suite where youngsters can have their own "bedroom in the sky" and daydream as they gaze over the Helena Valley. The coffeecake appeals to child and adult alike.

Caramel Apple Coffee Cake

2 cups flour
¼ cup sugar
2 teaspoons baking powder
¼ teaspoon salt
½ cup butter or margarine
1/3 cup milk
1 large egg, slightly beaten
1 medium apple, peeled, cored, diced

Topping:
¾ cup brown sugar
¼ cup melted butter
1/3 cup rolled oats

In a large bowl, sift together flour, sugar, baking powder and salt. Cut in ½ cup butter with a pastry knife until crumbly. Combine milk and egg, stir into flour mixture until soft dough forms. Pat ½ of dough into bottom of a greased 8-inch square pan. Cover with apples. Pat remaining dough over apples. In a saucepan, mix melted butter, brown sugar and oats together. Pour over cake mixture. Bake at 375° F for 30 minutes until golden brown. Cool on wire rack for 10 minutes before cutting.

Host and Hostess: Tom Woodall and Cheryl Boid

Address and Contact Numbers:
1999 Euclid Avenue, Helena, MT 59601
1-800-956-1999, 1-400-449-7492
www.appletoninn.com
e-mail: appleton@ixi.net

Mountain Meadow Inn

Beyond the meadows, framed in the last amber and crimson of late fall, rise Mt. Ascension and Mt. Helena of the Rocky Mountains continental divide. Beyond the hills to the northeast, blue waters of the Missouri blend with the sky. Views from the **Moun-**

tain Meadow Inn Bed and Breakfast show a pristine meadow, full of

beauty and wildlife. The carefree shelter of this home lets you relax and forget the stressors of an outside world. The owners, Kathy and John Ramirez, note that sand hill cranes, rabbits, coyote, eagles, deer and fox can be seen in the protected prairie beyond the windows. The rooms at the extreme ends of this broad mansion are best for viewing wildlife. There are seven windows in each room.

The Mountain Meadow Inn was built in 1927 as a retirement home. Clay tiles and concrete mortar bind the exterior walls, the brick terrace and the

fireplaces. Though there are no records, it is probable that the bricks were made at the Archie Bray Foundation. The Archie Bray is a landmark only two miles from the Inn. It began as a brick factory in 1885. The Bray is now a nationally acclaimed ceramic arts center. Potters from Japan, Europe and various parts of the United States learn

the art and functional intricacies of working with clay. Guests from the Mountain Meadow Inn take advantage of the tours and activities at the Bray.

The Mountain Meadow Inn has a variety of accommodations. It honors discounts for state and federal travelers. The restaurant has a full service license and a catering service and is available by reservation if you need multiple-day conference arrangements. Weddings and other festive ceremonies can be booked at the Inn.

Host and Hostess: John and Kathy Ramirez
Address and Contact Numbers:
2245 Head Lane, Helena, MT 59602
1-888-776-6466, 1-406-443-7301
Location:
The Inn is north of Highway 12 West. At the west end of Helena, turn right on Joslyn, fork left to Country Club Avenue. Go one mile and turn right at the Mountain Meadow sign on Head Lane. Go one mile to the Inn, marked by a sign and stone gates.

From Bannocks to Bundt Cake

The sights and sounds of many activities mark the route along the Jefferson River and the Three Forks area. Eager fishers populate the streams. Panning for gold, visiting local potters and lunching at Wheat Montana Bakery can take a day. Or, you can hike in the hills and explore the old mining gulches along Highway 15 between Helena and Butte.

The book, Montana Pay Dirt: A Guide to the Mining Camps of the Treasure State *by M. S. Wolle is helpful to persons interested in exploring old mining sites and their history. Wolle writes about camps that have disintegrated in the wind and weather. If you use your imagination, the sagging barnboard and rotting wagon wheels can resurrect voices and scenes from the not-too-distant past. The sourdoughs and hired ranch hands oftentimes carried sweet rolls in their pocket to munch on. The biscuits were rock hard and called "bannocks."*

The cheap way to mine gold was the panning method. The quick way to mine gold was the placer method. The expensive and arduous method to extract silver, zinc, copper and lead from metal-rich ore was done by smelters in Germany and Wales. Ore was shipped overseas until smelters like the Anaconda Company were established.

Butte, Montana, with its antiques shops and Old World architecture, is worth another day of investigation. Butte's charm is in its diversity. In the downtown area, a mixture of the elegant and the ribald exist. The Uptown Cafe and the Helsinki Bar represent two extremes. The specialty of the recently established Renaissance Bakery is its ethnic baked goods; they serve bundt cakes, not bannocks, with a choice of specialty coffees.

Petite Buttermilk Bundt Cake

4 large egg yolks
1/3 cup buttermilk
1½ teaspoons vanilla
2 cups sifted cake flour
1 cup sugar
1 teaspoon baking powder
½ teaspoon salt
8 tablespoons soft unsalted butter

Cinnamon Sugar Topping:
1 cup sugar
1 tablespoon cinnamon
½ cup melted butter

Mix topping sugar and cinnamon. Melt topping butter and set aside. In a medium bowl, combine the yolks, ¼ of the buttermilk and vanilla. In a large bowl combine the dry ingredients and blend with a mixer on low for 30 seconds. Add the soft butter and the remainder of the buttermilk to the dry ingredients and blend enough to moisten. Turn to medium speed on mixer, high for hand mixer. Beat, timing for exactly 1½ minutes. Add the egg and buttermilk mixture in three batches. Beat for exactly 20 seconds after each addition, scraping down the sides of the bowl each time. Spray or grease a

6-section nonstick mini-bundt pan or use 9x12-inch cake pan that is greased, bottom-lined with waxed or parchment paper, greased and floured again. Fill pans ½ full. For mini-bundts bake at 350°F for 20 minutes or until tester comes out clean. For 9-inch pan bake at 350°F for 30-40 minutes. For mini-bundts, invert on wire rack. Turn so tops are up. For pan, cool for 10 minutes, loosen the sides, and invert on rack. Cool completely. When cooled brush sides and top of cakes with melted butter. Coat the top and sides of the cakes twice by holding cake in one hand and using the other hand to pour cinnamon sugar over cake.

Owners: Janet Kozusko and Shirley Fields
Address and Contact Numbers:
Renaissance Baking Company
127 North Main, Butte, MT 59701
1-406-782-5536

Copper King Mansion

Butte's **Copper King Mansion Bed and Breakfast** is privately owned by the Coté family. It is a museum and a bed and breakfast home of ex-

traordinary quality. The King of the Copper Kings, William Andrews Clark, built the mansion in 1884. The era of the Copper Kings fascinates Montanans and tourists alike. The feud of Clark and Marcus Daly, the other noted Copper King, extended to the political and financial arena. However, it is the

Coté who have preserved the home so we can fully enjoy Butte as it was at the turn of the century.

The Copper King is open year-round as a bed and breakfast. Through the summer there are daily tours on the hour. Gabriel Offutt and Kory Silva are among the young guides who take pride in their Butte heritage. Their youthful viewpoint about the rise and fall of Senator Clark is engaging. A single tour is not adequate to absorb all of the interesting details of the mansion. For instance, German-born wood carvers created the intricacies on the fireplace. Muted frescos on the ceiling of the reception room help you appreciate attention to detail and preservation. The stained glass windows have retained their color. A full measure of sunshine enriches their detail if you stand on the second-story landing to view them.

The Master Suite, as its name indicates, was William Clark's private bordeaux. A sitting room replete with a carved mantle of bird's-eye maple, drapes of French appliqué and furniture of Victorian vintage are used as they were at the turn of the century. A beer stein collection adds interesting detail. The suite has a private bath.

Rooms named for Clark's daughters, Andree and Huguette, are also on the second floor. One room is large and golden with light; the other is cozier with rose hues. Each has a private sink; they share the shower of the century. The surround-sound shower is worth a stay at the Copper King. Turn it on and a million pinholes surging jets of warm water

make your skin tingle. It is dubbed the "human car wash." The mosaic of marble tiles in this bathroom is original to the building date. And there is an ancient ozone inhaler purported to cure baldness.

In the olden days, there were festivities each October 16 to celebrate French Butte's Lafayette Day. French Onion Soup as presented by Ann Coté Smith was the order of the day. A recipe for that soup is found in the *Butte Heritage Cookbook* and included here.

Copper King Cheese and Bacon Quiche

Pie crust for 8-inch springform pan:
2 cups flour
$1/_3$ cup margarine
½ teaspoon salt
4-5 tablespoons water

In medium bowl, sift flour and
salt, cut in margarine until crumbly. Gather into ball using water
to make crumbly dough stick
together. Roll between two
squares of waxed paper to a
round that will line a pie pan
completely or line a springform pan within ½ inch of edge.

Filling:
1 pound of bacon, fried and crumbled
1 pound shredded Swiss cheese
$1/_3$ cup finely chopped onion
4 eggs
2 cups whipping cream
¾ teaspoons salt
¼ teaspoon pepper
½ teaspoon ground red pepper

Combine bacon, cheese and onion; place in pastry-lined pie pan or spring-
form pan. Beat eggs lightly and add remaining ingredients. Beat until well
blended. Pour egg mixture over other contents. Bake at 350°F for 1 hour;
test. If quiche is still soft in middle, add 15 minutes baking time or bake until
tester comes out clean. Let stand for 10 minutes and cut into wedges.
Serve with fruit.

French Onion Soup

1½ pounds (5 cups) thinly sliced yellow onions
3 tablespoons butter
1 teaspoon sugar
3 tablespoon flour
2 quarts boiling beef stock
1 tablespoon oil
1 teaspoon salt
½ cup dry white wine or dry vermouth
3 tablespoons cognac
rounds of hard-toasted French bread
1-2 cups grated Swiss or Parmesan cheese

Cook onions with butter and oil slowly on low in a covered saucepan for 15 minutes. Uncover, raise heat to medium and stir in salt and sugar. Cook for 30-40 minutes stirring often until the onions have turned a deep golden brown. Sprinkle in flour and stir for 3 minutes. Remove from heat and blend into boiling liquid. Add the wine or vermouth and season to taste. Simmer partially covered for 30-40 minutes. Skim occasionally, correct seasoning. Just before serving, add cognac. Pour into soup tureen or separate soup bowls over bread rounds. Sprinkle with cheese.

Toast Rounds:
Take 12-16 slices of French bread cut 1-inch thick. Place in a roaster pan, 1 layer deep. Bake at 325°F for ½ hour or until brown and dried out. Halfway through the baking, baste each side with a teaspoon of olive oil or beef drippings. Spread each side with grated Parmesan and brown under broiler.

Host and Hostess: John Thompson and Erin Thompson Sigl
Address and Contact Numbers:
219 West Granite, Butte, MT 59701
1-406-782-7580

Iron Wheel

The iron wheel is symbolic to Sherry and John Cargill. Wagons on the grounds of the **Iron Wheel Bed and Breakfast** include carts, drays, sheep-herder wagons, Conestogas, chuck wagons and perhaps even a honey wagon or two. Horses and wheels have marked time on their ranch road since 1904 because it was the main route between Butte and Dillon. At the site of the old barn on the Cargill Ranch stood a boarding house where people stopped for the night.

The Cargills offer many arrangements for enjoying the Pipestone Creek and environs. Beside the bed and breakfast, they offer packages for big game hunts, floats or fishing trips, youth camps and trail riding. John is also a taxidermist. Sherry and John built the home to house their many activities and interests, and to provide two bedrooms with private baths and three with two shared bathrooms. The rooms are simple, clean and restful. When you are a guest of the Cargills you will be busy fishing, sightseeing or enjoying their sixty acres that sprawl along both sides of Pipestone Creek which flows through their ranch property. Full breakfasts are hardy; all meals are available upon request. Sherry cooks for the bed and breakfast and for the youth camps. That is how she knows that Tex-Mex is a favorite snack and Island Spareribs are a popular main dish.

Tex-Mex

Sour Cream Dressing:
1 cup sour cream
2 teaspoons taco seasoning
$1/3$ cup Miracle Whip

Dip:
Layer the following on a large platter in the order listed:
2 10-ounce cans of refried beans
1 large carton of guacamole or
two large avocados, peeled and pureed
sour cream mixture
3 medium tomatoes, diced
1 can sliced black olives
1 bunch green onions, chopped
8 ounces shredded cheddar cheese

Blend ingredients for sour cream mixture, set aside. Prepare and layer the ingredients for the tex-mex dip. Note that one of the layers is the sour cream dressing. May be served with fritos, chips. This recipe is a favorite of teenagers.

Island Spare Ribs

3 pounds spare ribs, browned
¼ cup vinegar
1 cup pineapple
3 tablespoons soy sauce
½ cup brown sugar
2 tablespoons cornstarch
1 teaspoon salt
½ green pepper, sliced

Trim and brown spare ribs; drain extra fat. Combine all other ingredients in a saucepan, mix thoroughly and bring to a boil; pour over ribs. Bake at 300°F for 2 hours.

Host and Hostess: John and Sherry Cargill

Address and Contact Numbers

40 Cedar Hills Road, Whitehall, MT 59759

1-406-494-2960 www.recworld.com/cargill

e-mail: joncargill@aol.com

Alder Gulch

Meriweather Lewis and William Clark explored the Three Forks area. The confluence of three rivers, the Jefferson, the Gallatin and the Madison form the headwaters of the Missouri within sight of the Tobacco Root Mountains. A half-century later, gold was found in the waters of those same foothills. However, Lewis and Clark were not looking for gold; they were looking for horses because the headwaters of the Missouri were not wide enough to navigate by boat or pirogue. And they were not looking for gold because their eyes were set on a destiny, that of finding a waterway to bind the western reaches of the Louisiana Purchase to the United States.

Alder Gulch was a focal point of Montana history in the making when gold was discovered there in 1863. Virginia City and Nevada City grew around Alder Gulch. By the turn of the century, other mining booms had stolen the population of Alder Gulch. Buildings in Virginia City and Nevada City were abandoned.

Fortunately, Virginia City survived. Not wind nor fire, not vandal nor varmint has destroyed the twenty-six stone and pine structures that stand along Alder Gulch. Moreover, Virginia City, though it could have been a ghost town, has never completely lost its population. There are always about a hundred hearty Montanans ready to swap stories, even in the dead of winter.

In 1949, the Congress of the United States created the National Trust for Historic Preservation and empowered the Trust to administer historical landmarks. In 1961, Virginia City was declared such a landmark. Were it not for the efforts of the Charles A. Bovey family, Virginia City would have disintegrated long before its designation as a landmark. Acting on a sense of pride in the rich history of this placer gold-mining site, Charles Bovey purchased and began restoring Virginia City's Alder Gulch in the 1930's.

Charles Bovey did not stop with a coat of varnish and a few lodge pole stabilizers. He continued with a whimsy that captivates the child in all of us. The shops and stores, the nooks and crannies came alive again. Portly shopkeepers, old-time sourdoughs and ladies of fashion stood in mannequin attention so we could see how the Virginians and the Vigilantes worked and played in the ribaldry of the Gold Rush.

By the 1970's the monumental task of keeping up with restoration was waning. However, with a revival in the art of preservation, Montanans are resurrecting Virginia City and Nevada City again. At the bend on Alder Gulch, an Interpretive Center is growing; the life-sized dolls which are mothballed will come back into action. Our children will see candles made from beeswax, hear sourdoughs in thick mackinaws swapping stories around a pot-bellied stove and taste pickles plucked fresh from the foamy brine of a grocer's pickle barrel.

Just An Experience

First-hand historical experience will come your way with a stay at Nevada City's **Just An Experience Bed and Breakfast**. Nevada City and Vir-

ginia City are extensions of each other. The northern section of Nevada City has vintage buildings salvaged from other places in Montana. Because John and Karma Sinerius grew up in Montana, they know the history of the state and the significance of Nevada City's restoration. John and Karma single-handedly supply many of the commercial interests in this tiny town. They have Star Bakery and Restaurant on main street, a large home for their bed and breakfast friends and their seasonal gift shop by the tourist train depot is open during the summer months.

The log house that stood at the site of what is now Just An Experience, was built in 1864. It is incorporated in John and Karma's new cedar home. A combination of rustic and natural accents blend well in each room. You can request a room with a private bath or you can ask about the fully

equipped cabins beyond the house. The cabins are spacious with a sleeping loft, kitchen, living room with a television and a master bedroom with a queen bed. The Sineriuses can provide information about scenic and historical places for good photos or they can take you on a photo shoot around the valley. Garnet and gold panning are on the agenda. The following recipes are family favorites.

Scampi in Porto Sauce

¼ cup whipping cream
6 tablespoons ketchup
¼ cup port wine
1 tablespoon cornstarch
½ teaspoon salt
½ teaspoon pepper
1 tablespoon olive oil
1 small clove crushed garlic
½ small onion, diced
1½ pounds large shrimp (scampi), shelled
and cleaned

In a double boiler, heat the cream and catsup to boiling temperature. Mix port with
cornstarch. Add slowly to simmering cream
mixture. Bring to a boil and thicken, stirring
constantly to prevent sticking. Add seasonings. Set aside. In a skillet,
sauté onion in olive oil. Add scampi and garlic. Heat until scampi turn pink;
do not overcook. Pour sauce over scampi and serve on rice.

Grandma Jean's Rolls

1 cup milk
½ cup water
2 teaspoons yeast
1 teaspoon baking powder
1/3 cup oil
½ teaspoon salt
1 egg, beaten
1/3 cup sugar
4-5 cups flour

Dissolve 2 teaspoons yeast in ½ cup warm water; set aside. Sift together
baking powder, salt and sugar; set aside. Scald milk, add oil and cool to
lukewarm. Combine with egg, dissolved yeast and sugar mixture. Stir in

3½ cups flour. Turn onto floured board, combine with remaining flour until soft. Knead and let rise in warm place until doubled. Punch down. Let rise again. Punch down and form into rolls. Let rise. Bake at 350°F for 20 minutes or until golden brown.

Host and Hostess: John and Karma Sinerius
Address and Contact Numbers:
1570 Highway 287, Virginia City, MT 59755
1-406-843-5402
www.bbhost.com./anexperience

Bennett House Country Inn

Karla Boyd, Nancy Allen and George Main are the new owners of Virginia City's **Bennett House Country Inn Bed and Breakfast**. Their voca-
tions blend perfectly for a suc-
cessful business. George is
death on dirt; he enjoys keeping
the lawns trim and the Victorian
home painted and tidy. Karla is
the technical brain of the group;
she does the marketing and the
advertising. Nancy is a designer
and hairdresser. She says, "It is
fun to nurture people in a posi-
tive way. We want to create a retreat that takes the words 'mundane' or
'hectic' out of a traveler's vocabulary."

Alton J. Bennett, whose name you will note on Virginia City's restored Hall
and Bennett House of Banking, had the home built in 1879. Intricately
carved woodwork is only one of the interior's attractive Victorian hallmarks.
Combine wood hues with carefully selected antiques, bright stained glass
windows and vivid wall colors and you will feel the comfort and vitality of
the Bennett House. Idaho Street can be your point of reference for finding
places in Virginia City; everything is within walking distance. The Brewery

and the Opera House present vaudeville slap-
stick and melodramas during the summer
months.

If you are a person who enjoys detail, look
through the stained glass window pictured
here. The house across the street was owned
by barrister W. F. Sanders in the time of the
Vigilantes.

In the morning, you can find the kitchen by
the "maid's entry" or through the unique
pocket doors. Either way there is always a

cheery cup of tea or a friendly cup of coffee brewing. A full breakfast is part of your stay at the Bennett House.

Little Smokies Casserole

1½ pound little smokies sausage, parboiled to remove grease
¾ cup chopped onions
¾ cup chopped mushrooms
8 slices cubed bread
1½ cups grated cheddar cheese
2¼ cups milk
4 eggs, slightly beaten
¾ teaspoon dry mustard
¼ cup chopped chives
1 can mushroom soup

Brown sausage, drain. Sauté mushrooms and onion. Mix bread, 1 cup cheese, milk, eggs, mustard, chives and soup. Add sausage, onions, and mushrooms. Grease 9x13-inch pan and fill with mixed ingredients. Refrigerate overnight. Bake 1 hour at 350°F. Top with remaining cheese the last 15 minutes of baking. Cool for 10 minutes, cut and serve.

Host and Hostesses: George Main, Karla Boyd, Nancy Allen
Address and Contact Numbers:
115 East Idaho Street, Virginia City, MT 59755
1-877-843-5220, 1-406-843-5220
www.bennetthouseinn.com

Stonehouse Inn

John and Linda Hamilton have operated the **Stonehouse Inn Bed and Breakfast** for almost a decade. The square timbers and local granite make the Stonehouse a natural monument to Virginia City. The view
from the front porch is reminiscent of a scene from "The Gun-
fight at OK Corral," especially
if you consider that Boot Hill is
only a piece down the road. The
Tobacco Roots barely peak
above the Ruby Valley. The hills
can be dry and dusty with a
bundle of sagebrush rolling along

with the jackrabbits. Man and beast, tourist and landrover, find respite in
the coulee of the Ruby River under the willows or leaning against a cottonwood

Politics and mining are dear to the heart of the Hamiltons; Linda looks at
Virginia City's best interests and sees the golden age of tourism just around

the corner. She is a former
mayor of Virginia City. On the
other hand, preserving the liveli-
hood of mining and farming is
important, too. John has always
been a miner and respects the
mining interests of the Ruby Valley. Gold and garnets, talc, mica
and silver are elements from
the valley that have contributed
to Montana's economy over the
last two centuries.

A blacksmith, George Thexton, built the Stonehouse. The Hamiltons are its
third owners and their electrical and plumbing updates have not changed the

historical flavor of the guest areas. The large dining room is warm and inviting especially decked out in Linda's stencils. New coverlets on antique brass beds complete an essence of the past. Coupled with an excursion to Nevada City on a narrow-gauge tour train or a narrated ride through town to Boot Hill in a horse and buggy, you get a glimpse of Virginia City's colorful past.

Sylvia Shaw's Baking Powder Biscuits

3 cups flour
2 tablespoons sugar
4½ teaspoons baking powder
¾ teaspoon cream of tartar
¾ teaspoon salt
¾ cup lard
1 egg
1 cup buttermilk

Mix dry ingredients, cut in lard, beat in egg and milk. Knead 15 times, roll out ¾-inch thick. Cut and bake at 400°F for 12 minutes.

Host and Hostess: John and Linda Hamilton
Address and Contact Numbers:
306 East Idaho Street, Virginia City, MT 59755
1-406-843-5504

9T9

9T9 Ranch Bed and Breakfast and Judy's Table Restaurant are located on the Madison River. Famous for blue-ribbon trout fishing, a bend of the Madison River runs below the house. You feel like you are on top of the world; views extend about fifty miles into the distance, yet the Madison River flows just below the gate of the 9T9.

There is no shortage of activities to keep you busy at 9T9. Judy has embellished all three guestrooms with unique home-spun details corresponding to the name of the room. Wreaths in the Bunkhouse Room are of barbed wire and boots. In the Madison Room, details for the fisher abound, and the Country Room has a peacock feather and floral arrangement. All have queen or twin beds and a private bath.

Ennis is in the heart of fishing and mountain climbing country. It is also close to attractions like Virginia City and Nevada City with their history of the Gold Rush era. Yellowstone Park can be on your itinerary with a delicious meal to follow at Judy's Table. On warm summer evenings, chuck wagon dinners and eating by the campfire are typical Montana pastimes.

Seafood Sauté with Herb Butter

Herb Butter:
1 cup butter
? teaspoon white pepper
¼ teaspoon tarragon
¼ tablespoon chervil (basil)
¼ tablespoon parsley
¼ cup chopped green onions

Seafood Sauté:
1½ ounces herb butter
5 ounces scallops
2 large shrimp, sliced in half lengthwise
1½ ounces Dungeness crab
½ cup white wine (Chablis)

Use only a portion of prepared herb butter; save the rest. Melt herb butter
in pan on medium heat. Add scallops and cook about 3 minutes or until
scallops are turning white. Add remaining ingredients and simmer 4 to 5
minutes longer or until shrimp turns pink.
Serve immediately.

Hostess: Judy Herrick
Address and Contact Numbers:
Box 564, 99 Gravelly Range Road, Ennis, MT 59729
1-800-484-5862, 1-406-682-7659, www.moscow.com/business/9t9ranch
e-mail: jherrick@3rivers.net
Location:
From Ennis take Highway 287 going west toward Virginia City. Go two miles to
signs pointing to Varney Road and Fish Hatchery to left. Take road for 7 miles to
intersection with Gravelly Range Road. Go straight for 1 mile to 9T9.

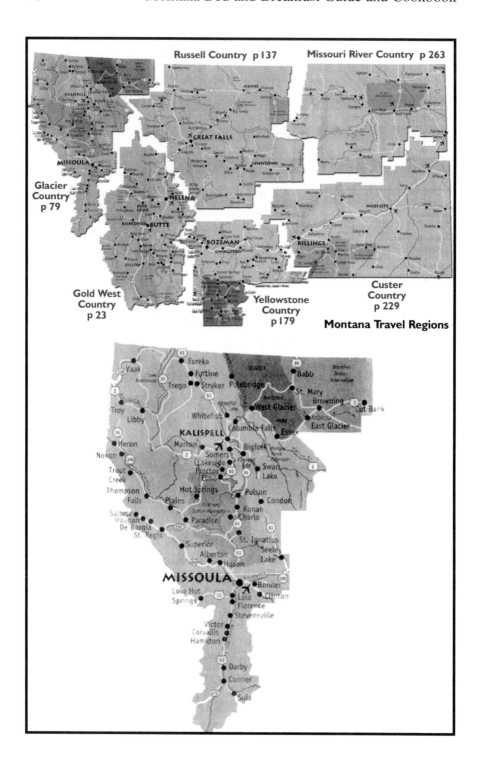

Russell Country p 137

Missouri River Country p 263

Glacier Country p 79

Gold West Country p 23

Yellowstone Country p 179

Custer Country p 229

Montana Travel Regions

Glacier Country

The wilderness of Skalkaho pass in southwestern Montana separates Gold West Country and Glacier Country. The flora changes. Crimson sheep laurel and Indian paint brush beside deep purple flax and mountain lupine contrast with pastel bitterroot and wild roses. Mist, like inverted rain, collects at the bottom of the waterfall that pours from the Sapphire Mountains. Take a deep breath in this mountain mist and get ready to travel to the Blue Mountains of the Bitterroot Valley. The Bitterroot Valley offers areas for hiking, biking, canoeing, golfing, cross-country skiing, snowmobiling, fishing and birdwatching.

Deer Crossing

Evening grosbeak chatter a pleasant welcome to guests at the **Deer Crossing Bed and Breakfast**. The pine, aspen and cottonwoood at Deer Crossing provide a refuge to a variety of birds, making this home a birder's paradise. There are downy and pileated woodpecker, mountain finch, pine siskin, crossbill, rufous and Calliope hummingbirds, nut hatches, killdeer, heron, raven, bald eagles and magpie.

Deer Crossing's Western theme is appropriate to its wide-open spaces. Rooms like the Charlie Russell have willow wicker furniture and are rich in artistic detail. Like the Annie Oakley Room, they

portray an aspect of Montana's heritage. Surrounding the original homestead, called the Bunkhouse, are flowering crab and lilac.

Home economist turned cowgirl, Mary Lynch is a pretty hostess with lots of energy. Your breakfast will come from her cookbook, *Deer Crossing's Pantry of Recipes*. Mary's Rum Bundt Cake is delicious as a dessert or as a pick-me-up at any time of the day.

Rum Bundt Cake

Dough:
1 package yellow cake mix
1 small packet instant, uncooked vanilla pudding
½ cup oil
¼ cup rum
½ cup water
1 teaspoon vanilla
4 eggs
½ cup chopped walnuts

Combine cake mix and vanilla pudding. Add oil, rum, water and vanilla. Add eggs one at a time and beat well after each egg. Grease and flour a bundt pan and sprinkle chopped nuts at the bottom. Pour in batter and bake at 325°F for 1 hour. During the last 5 minutes of baking, boil the following ingredients:

Topping:
½ cup of butter
¼ cup sugar
Remove from heat and add:
2 tablespoons rum

Poke holes in the cake with a fork while it is still in pan. Pour the heated rum mixture slowly over the cake. Cool, remove from pan and serve.

Hostess: Mary Lynch
Address and Contact Numbers:
396 Hayes Creek Road, Hamilton, MT 59840
1-800-763-2232, 1-406-363-2232
www.wtp.net/go/deercrossing
e-mail: deercros@bitterroot.net
Location:
Go fifty miles south of Missoula on Highway 93. At Hayes Creek Road turn right and go 1.5 miles to 396 Hayes Creek Road.

Trout Springs

Trout Springs Bed and Breakfast is a country estate located on a fen of the Bitterroot River. Maynard and Brenda Gueldenhaar have parlayed active vocational careers into an avocation. A small gift shop, an intimate restaurant with a sunny deck and a luxu-

rious room with a private bath rise to the expectations of the most discriminating traveler.

As the name implies, the stream flowing through the yard of this bed and breakfast is stocked so you can catch your own trout for breakfast. The gift shop is stocked too. Ornamental ironworks are the unique handiwork of your host. He creates candleholders, towel racks, lamps, headboards, tables and mirror frames. Brenda sells cookbooks, robes and T-shirts. She fashions lampshades and ornamental teepees from rawhide. You will see these items used with artistic flair in the guest areas. All bedrooms have king beds and private bathrooms.

As a guest at Trout Springs, you have the opportunity to sample the variety of foods featured in Brenda's cookbook Here are two delicious recipes.

Chicken Vegetable Bundles Supreme

3 whole chicken breasts, skinned and cut in half
3 tablespoons butter or margarine, melted
2 carrots julienned (cut 4 inches x $1/_8$ inch x $1/_8$ inch)
1 medium zucchini julienned (cut 4 inches x $1/_8$ inch x $1/_8$ inch)
½ teaspoon salt
¼ teaspoon crushed rosemary
¼ teaspoon pepper
6 slices bacon
½ cup chicken broth

Sauce:
½ cup chicken broth
½ cup sour cream
1 tablespoon flour

Flatten chicken breasts to about ¼-inch thickness by pounding between sheets of waxed paper. In a bowl, combine butter, carrots, zucchini, salt, rosemary and pepper. Divide mixture evenly between each flattened chicken breast. Roll up chicken breast. Wrap 1 bacon slice around each chicken bundle and secure with colored toothpick. Place the chicken bundles in a 9x13-inch baking dish. Pour chicken broth over chicken.

Preheat oven to 350°F. Bake, basting occasionally for 35 to 40 minutes or until chicken is tender. Place chicken bundles on platter. Reserve pan juices plus enough chicken broth to equal ¼ cup. In a small bowl stir together sour cream and flour. Stir into juice mixture. Cook over medium heat, stirring occasionally, until thickened. DO NOT BOIL. Serve over chicken bundles. Serves 4-5.

Spicy Baked Pears with Yogurt

5 large ripe pears
½ cup dark brown sugar
¾ cup orange juice
¼ cup butter
cinnamon
nutmeg
cloves
vanilla yogurt

Slice pears in half, remove core and stem. Line bottom of glass baking dish with brown sugar. Lay pears, cut side down, on sugar. Pour orange juice over pears and dot with butter. Sprinkle generously with cinnamon, nutmeg and a pinch of cloves. Bake at 350°F for 20-30 minutes or until pears are tender. Serves 8-10.

To serve, place pear, cut side down in a serving dish. Pour some of the brown sugar and orange juice mixture over the pears and top with a dollop of vanilla yogurt. NOTE: This can be prepared in advance by combining all the ingredients except the orange juice. Pour over just before baking.

Host and Hostess: Maynard and Brenda Gueldenhaar

Address and Contact Numbers:
721 Desta Street, Hamilton, MT 59840
1-888-678-7688, 1-406-375-0911
www.wtp.net/go/troutsprings
e-mail: Tsprings@bitterroot.net

Big Creek Pines

Big Creek Pines Bed and Breakfast is a holiday spot for the vacationing homemaker. Hostess Rosemary Beason brings creative skills to life in the clean detail and variety of each room. For instance, Rosemary's stencils add bold burgundy, blue, and green accents in the Huckleberry Room. The duvets match the decor. The green hues of the Aspen Room are like the thicket along the riverbank just below your window seat. The fishing is excellent on the Bitterroot River, and fishers will not be content to watch the wilderness from a window seat.

Big Creek Pines was built as a bed and breakfast home. All of the rooms overlook the river. Individual thermostats give guests control of the temperature in their own room. A third floor conference area is available for small gatherings or seminars. A cozy fireplace keeps the dining area warm in winter. In summer a deck flooded with early morning light is used to serve breakfast. Fresh cookies and milk are available for midday snacks and Apple-Rice Pudding Pie is tasty for breakfast or dessert.

Apple-Rice Pudding Pie

Rice Crust:
1½ cups warm cooked rice
3 tablespoons melted butter

Butter a deep 9-inch pie or quiche dish.
With back of spoon, press the warm rice
into the dish and drizzle with melted butter. Bake at 350°F for 5 minutes. Crust
can be used ½ hour after baking or covered and refrigerated overnight.

Apple Filling:
3 Granny Smith apples, peeled, diced
½ cup brown sugar
2½ teaspoons cinnamon
1 cup half-and-half
3 eggs, beaten
scant cup of shredded Monterey Jack cheese

Preheat oven to 400ºF. In the rice prepared dish, spread apples evenly
on top of rice. Sprinkle with brown sugar and cinnamon. Beat together the cream and eggs, add cheese and pour over apples, making
sure all apples are covered. Bake for approximately 50 minutes or
until the center of the pie is set. Remove from oven and let sit for 15
minutes before slicing. Serves 6. For pretty presentation, slice an
unpeeled red apple into ¼ inch slices. Dip in lemon juice and lay 2
slices of apple and a mint leaf on top of each slice.

Host and Hostess: Joe and Rosemary Beason
Address and Contact Numbers:
2986 Highway 93 North, Stevensville, MT 59870
1-888-300-6475, 1-406-642-6475, www.wtp.net/go/bigcreek
e-mail: bcpl@cybernetl.com
Location:
Twenty-seven miles south of Missoula. B&B sign is between mile markers 62 and
63 on Highway 93.

Mystical Mountain

The stately pines swaying slowly in the prairie wind at the **Mystical Mountain Bed and Breakfast** cast a sense of serenity over the countryside. They witnessed the ancient ritual of the Nez Perce Indians on their trek to summer camp in the Bitterroot Valley. They sensed the tranquility of this Native American band communing with the land and called it good.

The windows of the great room at Mystical Mountain look upon the valley. The southern exposure bathes you in light especially if you view the stone fireplace and spacious common area from the balcony near the 30-foot vaulted ceiling.

Chef Jan Adams-Grant, owner of Mystical Mountain Bed and Breakfast and Restaurant, is a geophysicist. A career change brought her to culinary school. Grant's restaurant serves the valley and her private guests. Jan is acclaimed for her delicious homemade breads. Examples are Gabriel bread, cheese-stuffed fry bread, bread pudding and Montana toast, which is flattened bread dough, dipped in egg batter, deep-fried to golden perfection and served with syrup. Eggs and bread pudding are featured here.

Mystical Mountain Eggs Southwestern

4 tablespoons butter
2 tablespoons flour
1 cup chicken stock
5 tablespoons Gruyere cheese
½ cup cubed cooked chicken
½ cup sliced button mushrooms
2 teaspoons pimiento
2 teaspoons Hungarian paprika
1 teaspoon Worcestershire sauce
1 teaspoon celery salt
2 pinches cayenne (optional, add carefully)
butter for ramekins
6 eggs

In a sauce pan heat butter, blend in flour and slowly add stock. Stir in 4 tablespoons cheese. When melted add next 7 ingredients. Cook 5 minutes. Pour a portion of sauce in individual well-buttered ramekins. Add 1 egg each. Cover with remaining sauce, sprinkle with remaining cheese, and bake at 350°F for 10 minutes.

Bread Pudding

2 cups milk
¼ cup butter
½ cup sugar
1 teaspoon ground cinnamon
¼ teaspoon salt
2 large eggs, slightly beaten
6 cups dry breadcrumbs
½ cup raisins

Scald milk and melt butter in 2-quart pan over medium heat. Mix sugar, cinnamon, salt and eggs in large bowl with wire whisk until well blended. Stir in bread and raisins. Combine with milk mixture. Pour into ungreased 1 ½ quart casserole or square baking dish 8x8x2 inches. Place casserole in rectangular pan 13x9x2 inches. Pour hot water into rectangular pan until 1 inch deep. Bake uncovered at 350°F for 40-45 minutes or until knife inserted 1 inch from edge of casserole comes out cleanly. Cool ½ hour and drizzle with a topping of powdered sugar and water mixed to the consistency of whipping cream.

Hostess: Jan Adams-Grant
Address and Contact Numbers
126 Indian Prairie Loop, Stevensville, MT 59870
1-406-642-3464
Location:
28 miles south of Missoula on Highway 93.

Goldsmith's Inn

The story of **Goldsmith's Inn Bed and Breakfast** is a dream come true. Richard Goldsmith was one of twenty Missoula entrepreneurs to submit a plan for the restoration of a beautiful and historical home on the University of Montana Campus. Two important details are important to the story. First, the price of the house was its removal from the campus site. And second, the high quality of the other proposals made competition keen. From the twenty proposals, the selection committee found Goldsmith's plan to open a bed and breakfast the most resourceful. The Goldsmith's Inn Bed and Breakfast was born.

The mansion was moved in two pieces and stands in mid-town Missoula on the banks of the Clark Fork River. It was built in 1911 under the auspices of Clyde Duniway, the second president of the University of Montana. Goldsmith's has been in operation since 1990.

Jeana Goldsmith manages the interior decorating of this home. The house is tastefully detailed in a "Victorian tradition with modern day amenities." In fact, Goldsmith's caters to business and executive travelers who need telephones and computer jacks. However, if you really want to be out of the mainstream for a few days, choose one of the suites with a balcony that

overlooks the Clark Fork River. All of the Goldsmith's seven rooms have queen beds and private baths.

Attached to Goldsmith's, but secluded from it, is the restaurant that began as an ice cream business. It is the Waterfront Pasta House and Goldsmith's Ice Cream Parlour. Guests have a choice of items on the hearty breakfast menu when they are ready to begin the day.

Mediterranean Pasta Salad

8 oz. Penne pasta
4 quarts water
1 pound boneless skinless chicken breasts
$1/2$ tsp. chicken bouillon
$1/2$ cup diagonally cut green beans, steamed
1 can sliced pitted ripe olives
$1/4$ cup chopped fresh basil
1 cup cherry tomatoes

Cook pasta in 4 quarts of water. Poach chicken with $1/2$ tsp. bouillon in enough water to cover chicken breasts. Drain and cool pasta. Cool chicken breasts and cut into 2-inch pieces. Add tomatoes, olives, basil and green beans. Dress with a bottled Italian dressing.

Host and Hostess: Richard and Jeana Goldsmith
Address and Contact Numbers:
809 East Front Street, Missoula, MT 59801
1-406-721-6732
www.goldsmithsinn.com

Foxglove Cottage

The **Foxglove Cottage Bed and Breakfast** was originally part of a farmstead on Rattlesnake Creek in the Missoula Valley. The cottage farmhouse was abandoned after the sale of the farmland. Today it is beautifully restored and cared for by hosts, John Keegan and Anthony Cesare.

This cottage bed and breakfast is intimate and peaceful with an abundance of gourmet food. The Foxglove boasts a catering service for special occasions. A profusion of colors mark the tulip, petunia, poppy and flowering crab of early spring. The side yard breaks into an immense three-tiered Victorian garden. Foxglove and other perennials, annuals, climbing vine, flowering shrubs and evergreens almost hide the tidy cottage which has two guestrooms. A swimming pool and a sense of the European homestay give the Foxglove Cottage distinction.

Hosts: John Keegan and Anthony Cesare
Address and Contact Numbers:
2331 Gilbert Avenue, Missoula, MT 59802
1-406-543-2927

Cougar Ranch Inn

The **Cougar Ranch Inn Bed and Breakfast** is new to Glacier Country. It is located in the Evaro Valley, north of Missoula on Highway 93. The open-beam architecture and baseboard-to-ceiling windows give this home an abundance of light and space. You can sit in the sunken living room or on the north-facing deck and watch the sun set over the Mission Mountains. In the foreground, the meadowland is punctuated by small stands of lodgepole and Ponderosa pine.

The cross-cultural experiences offered at Cougar Ranch are unique. Helene is originally from France and fluent in French. She came to Missoula as a journalist. Her husband is a photographer who covers national and international news events. Helene's mother is an artist in two painting media, acrylic and watercolor. Her work will grace the walls of the Cougar.

This home has five bedrooms with private baths. Two of the baths have sunken whirlpool tubs. A taste of French hospitality and cuisine are a highlight of the Cougar. Apricot specialties are a summer favorite when this fruit is in season.

Host and Hostess: Alan Higbee and Helene Bourdon
Address and Contact Numbers:
Box 9431, Missoula, MT 59807
1-406-726-3745, 1-406-542-9348
e-mail: wnl@marsweb.com
Location:
North of Missoula on Highway 93, take a right just past mile marker 8.

Schoolhouse and Teacherage

The memories of old-fashioned school days with playground puppy love, lard bucket lunches, homemade paste, chalk dust and the anticipation of winter holidays are embodied in the creation of the **Schoolhouse and Teacherage Bed and Breakfast**.

Fall is a perfect time to visit the Schoolhouse and Teacherage Bed and Breakfast. You walk up the path to the old schoolhouse that is now the main house. The deep golden glow of changing birch leaves and the smell of apple cider elicit a blend of school memories - confining and liberating - by turn. As you ring the doorbell a crisp "gong" resounds from the bell tower, just as it did in 1901 when loggers' children from the surrounding area were called to their first day in a new schoolhouse.

The Family Ippisch, Hanneke and Les, host the Teacherage where sleeping is a memorable event. Every queen bed is of unique construction. The first layer is a box spring and accompanying mattress. Over this is a feather bed. The sheets, top and bottom, come next. Over the top sheet is a comforter and covering the comforter is a showy quilt top that is removed and folded on a quilt stand for the night.

Each room has a different theme. Hanneke is from Sweden so one room represents the Scandinavian tradition. A sheer, crisp white canopy shines over the headboard and the antique quilt of multicol-

ored rosettes. Les is a woodcrafter and has built wardrobes on each side of the bed.

The Amish Room is famous for its quilts. In the Montana Room are a mounted bobcat and mountain goat, common to the mountain terrain of Huson. Christmas colors vividly mark the Dutch room and also remind us that the Schoolhouse and Teacherage celebrates the Christmas season in a grand way. Over five thousand people attend the Christmas show where the nativity sets designed by Les and the books written by Hanneke are for sale. Orders are filled in time for Christmas.

The privacy of the cabin and Teacherage is balanced by the community spirit of breakfast in the main house. Hanneke serves a three-course breakfast. The first course is granola and huckleberries over home-made yogurt. The second course consists of a variety of breads and cheeses, and the last course is an applesauce pastry drenched in berry syrup and topped with whipping cream. Coffee, tea and juices complete the meal.

Host and Hostess: Les and Hanneke Ippisch

Address and Contact Numbers:
9 mile, Huson, MT 59846
1-406-626-5879

Location:
On I-90, 27 miles west of
Missoula, take exit 82. Go 1½
miles, take a right on Remount
Road. Go 1½ miles to distinctive
Polish fence.

Emily A

The Seeley Lake's **Emily A Bed and Breakfast** is located twenty miles north of the junction of Highways 200 and 83. The Emily A readily serves the Seeley-Swan-Kalispell area. At this location, travelers from Missoula, Helena and Great Falls find the Emily A handy as they take Highway 2 across Montana.

Keith and Marilyn Peterson represent fourth generation Montanans. Establishing an elegant yet rustic bed and breakfast has been a lifelong dream. Keith is a family physician and Marilyn is a dietician. As a guest at the Emily A, you feel pampered. A small library and walking trails encourage solitude and reflection. The 11,000 square feet of family and guest area include five rooms with private baths, a two-room family suite and eight bathrooms.

Artistic touches unique to the Emily A include original work of Marilyn's uncle Irvin "Shorty" Shope. Original art, posters and prints by artists Tucker Smith and Monte Dolack are enhanced by the native timbers of exposed log walls. A family of loons on the mantle remind you of the private lake and trails on the 160 acres of ranch and timber land that become yours to roam for a day, a week or even longer.

Marilyn uses her talents as a dietician when she caters luncheons and

dinners in the Emily A's conference center or when she serves breakfast and conversation to breakfast guests. *Cooking À Lá Heart* endorsed by the American Heart Association is one of her favorite cookbooks. This muffin recipe is worth sharing.

Blueberry Muffins

1 cup flour
1 cup whole wheat flour
½ cup plus ½ tablespoon sugar
1 tablespoon baking powder
½ teaspoon cinnamon
2 cups fresh or frozen blueberries
¼ cup margarine, melted
½ cup skim milk
1 egg
1 egg white
½ teaspoon vanilla

In a bowl combine flour, ½ cup sugar, baking powder and cinnamon. In a separate bowl, toss blueberries with 1 tablespoon of the flour mixture, set aside. Into melted margarine stir milk, egg, egg whites and vanilla. Add mixture to dry ingredients. Mix until well moistened. Stir in berries. Spoon batter into nonstick muffin tins. Sprinkle top with remaining ½ tablespoon sugar. Bake at 350°F for 15 minutes or until golden. Cool 5 minutes. Makes 12 muffins.

Host and Hostess: Keith and Marilyn Peterson

Address and Contact Numbers:
P.O. Box 350, Seeley Lake, MT 59868
1-800-977-4639, 1-406-677-FISH,
www.theemilya.com
e-mail: slk3340@montana.com
Location:
Highway 83 on the 20-mile marker, five miles north of Seeley Lake

Stoneheart Inn

The **Stoneheart Inn Bed and Breakfast** is located in historic St. Ignatius. It was originally built as a stagecoach stop and connected the Swan and Flathead Valleys. After different uses and owners, present owner and hostess, Judith Ellis-Tholt says, "It was meant to be a bed and breakfast home and serves locals and tourists alike." The Mission Mountains are at the doorstep of the Stoneheart with 89,500 acres and nine trailheads open to hikers.

The old-fashioned great room, refurbished in Early Americana, provides ample common space for dining and relaxing, playing games and reading. Antiques, pine primitives, conversation pieces and collectibles displayed throughout the house are for sale. The Stoneheart's location puts it within walking distance of the Flathead Indian Museum and the Mission trails.

The accommodations at the Stoneheart Inn are glorious because of the view of the Mission Mountain Range and the sweet dreams upon Montana's finest "Three Dog Down" comforters. All rooms have private baths and three have private sitting rooms as well. The rooms honor traditional aspects of the area with names like the Dream Catcher of the Native Americans, the Wilderness, the Bunkhouse of the Wild West and the Sweetheart, for the lover in all of us. Book a night soon and let Mike and Judith know which room is most suitable to your personality. Enjoy food like Twice the Guilt Cake without any guilt.

Twice the Guilt Cake

1 cup sugar
1 teaspoon vanilla
2 eggs
2 cups flour
1 teaspoon salt
1 teaspoon soda
13½ ounce can undrained crushed pineapple
½ cup brown sugar
½ cup coconut
½ cup chopped pecans

Sauce: Melt ½ cup butter, stir in ½ cup light cream, ½ cup sugar, and ½ teaspoon vanilla.

Combine sugar, vanilla and eggs. Beat 2 minutes at medium speed. At low speed add flour, salt, soda and pineapple. Mix 1 minute. Pour into greased 9x13-inch pan. Sprinkle mixture of brown sugar, coconut, and pecans on top. Bake at 350°F 30-35 minutes. Just before cake is done prepare sauce. Pour over warm cake. Cool and serve with whipped cream topping.

Host and Hostess: Mike and Judith Tholt
Address and Contact Numbers:
26 North Main, P.O. Box 236, St. Ignatius, MT 59865
1-800-866-9197, 1-406-745-4999
e-mail: sti4999@montana.com

Hawthorne House

Gerry and Karen (McIntire) Lenz open **Hawthorne House Bed and Breakfast** in Polson to guests all year. Karen is a teacher; reservations in advance of your stay are necessary during the school year. Karen was born and raised in Polson. She is an eager and accurate historian.

The story of the McIntires of Polson began in the early 1890's when owners of the Great Northern Railroad enticed people out west with the promise of tillable land. The McIntires traveled by train to Montana; their personal effects were in the boxcar, and the family traveled in the caboose. Twenty years later the Flathead Indian Reservation opened to white settlers. The McIntires established a hotel and trading post on Flathead Lake just blocks from the present site of Hawthorne House.

Artifacts, tools, clothing and dishes contribute to the displays at the

Hawthorne House. In one room is a collection of rich beaded jackets, leggings, moccasins and gloves that are among Karen's most treasured antiques. She recalls how her grandfather spoke with pride about his friends from the Salish-Kootenai tribe. In another room, a crocheted hat from the flapper era and a veiled black piece with a pheasant feather are on display. The kitchen wall holds a display of antique baking utensils and spices plus a hoosier baking center.

All rooms are furnished with family heirlooms. Gerry is a carpenter and his skilled handiwork is also a part of every room. Karen enjoys sewing and baking. Her breakfasts are an event celebrated each morning around a big friendly oak table. This favorite is easy because it blends overnight.

Refrigerator Eggs

2 3½-ounce cans chopped green chiles
1½ pounds fried sausage
1 pound grated cheese
½ cup chopped scallions
3 eggs
2 cups milk
½ cup Bisquick

Line 9x13-inch greased pan with chiles. Layer sausage, cheese and scallions. Whip eggs and milk, add Bisquick. Pour over layers. Refrigerate overnight. Bake at 350°F for 45 minutes. Allow to set for 15 minutes. Cut in squares and serve hot.

Host and Hostess: Gerry and Karen Lenz
Address and Contact Numbers:
304 Third Avenue East, Polson, MT 59860
1-406-883-2723

Burggraf's

In the thicket along a country lane overlooking Swan Lake and the Mission Mountains, R.J. and Natalie Burggraf created **Burggraf's Country Lane Bed and Breakfast** in 1984. The living room is the heart of this home and people and animals alike enjoy the sunshine and trailing vines that create an atmosphere of relaxation.

Note that you are contributing to the welfare of children in remote parts of the world with a stay at the Burggraf's. Each winter, Natalie takes a portion of her proceeds from the bed and breakfast and delivers school and medical supplies to children who are destitute. R.J. "keeps the homefires burning" while Natalie becomes the conduit to expand the horizons of people who may not have seen another American. She

"lives among the village people and eats with them. Her most memorable meal was bat stew; sweet and sour goldfish with roasted beetles runs a close second."

Burggraf's quiet lagoon has a mesmerizing effect. Stellar jays, robins, chickadees, rose-breasted grosbeak and camp robbers provide the entertainment around a game of lawn croquet on Burggraf's largest, groomed course in the Northwest. Inside, a choice of rooms with baths and queen or king beds offer a night of peaceful slumber. And in the morning, R.J.'s strong version of a wake-up call is ready as early as five-thirty for people with a business agenda. Later risers can awaken leisurely over this fine recipe contributed by Natalie.

Easy Step Ham Omelet

4 eggs
½ cup Bisquick mix
½ cup skim milk
1 teaspoon salt
1 tablespoon Worcestershire
sauce
2 tablespoons regular mustard
1 teaspoon garlic powder
½ teaspoon red pepper
2 medium zucchini, chopped
2 medium tomato, chopped
1 medium onion, chopped
1 cup shredded ham
1 cup shredded cheddar cheese

Heat oven to 325°F. Beat eggs slightly; beat in baking mix, milk, salt, Worcestershire sauce, garlic powder and red pepper. Layer zucchini, tomatoes, onion and ham in an ungreased 8x8x2-inch baking dish. Pour egg mixture over layered ingredients. Sprinkle with cheese. Bake uncovered until knife inserted one inch from top comes out clean, about 40-50 minutes. Let stand 15 minutes before cutting and serving with fresh fruit. Serves 4-6.

Host and Hostess: R.J. and Natalie Burggraf

Address and Contact Numbers:
Rainbow Drive, Bigfork, MT
59911
1-800-525-3344, 1-406-837-4608
e-mail: burggraf@digisys.net
Location:
Highway 209 to four corner
intersection. South ½ mile. Go to
Rainbow Drive. Turn right and go
3 miles to row of mail boxes. Stay
to right and go .7 of a mile to
Burggraf's.

O'Duachain Country Inn

The elegant **O'Duachain Country Inn Bed and Breakfast** speaks for the high, wide and handsome style of Montana. Replete with ponds and peacocks, it has the only wind dulcimer in Glacier Country.

O'Duachain, established in 1985, is currently owned by Mary and Bill Knoll. It recently received a high rating of "10" for cleanliness and service. From the first phone call to the last good-bye, Mary and Bill radiate a love of life and a homespun affection for people, a perfect combination for hosting a bed and breakfast business. As a guest you may choose the elegance of the main house dominated by the warmth of two massive fireplaces or the privacy of the two-story guest house.

Mary, who balances motherhood and the management of a bed and breakfast with a career in Washington, D.C., has the verve to do well in both arenas. The peace of O'Duachain through the eyes one of the

Knoll children is well put, "Mommy, if I knew we would be so beautiful, I would have let us move a long time ago." She came to O'Duachain as a two-year-old and is now five.

The O'Duachain's Western leprechauns stand at sentinel attention, greeting guests at the gate. The breakfast table is set with linen, china and crystal for the ethnic specialty Stuffed IrishToast.

O'Duachain Country Inn Stuffed IrishToast

1 loaf French bread

Filling:
 8 ounces cream cheese
1 teaspoon vanilla
¾ cup sliced almonds
¼ cup powdered sugar

Batter:
3 whole eggs
1 pint whipping cream

Topping:
2 jars apricot preserves
frozen, canned, or fresh blackberries (if canned drain juice).
fresh grated nutmeg

Toast almonds by heating in a small fry pan over medium heat, stirring often. Place the cream cheese in a glass bowl and warm in the micro-

wave to room temperature until soft. Add toasted almonds, vanilla and powdered sugar. Mix well. Cut loaf of French bread in 1 inch slices, then slice once again, but not all the way through, to make a pocket for the cream cheese mixture. Spread mixture inside the pockets using about a tablespoon for each slice. Dip slices into batter and fry on a hot griddle until brown. Use bacon grease for frying because it adds to the flavor of the toast. In the meantime, warm apricot preserves, blackberries and nutmeg in a small pan. Drizzle over toast and serve. Serves 4

Host and Hostess: Bill and Mary Knoll

Address and Contact numbers:
675 Ferndale Drive, Bigfork, MT 59911
1-800-837-7460, 1-406-837-0778
Location:
From Bigfork, take Highway 35 to Highway 209. Go east 3.5 miles to Ferndale Drive (Volunteer Fire Department will be on your left). Go left 1.5 miles to 675 Ferndale Drive.

Coyote Roadhouse

The **Coyote Roadhouse Inn Bed and Breakfast** includes a Mobil three-star restaurant. Gary Hastings' Inn successfully exemplifies the Western roadhouse of yesteryear. You can imagine a stagecoach arriving at the doorstep of the

Roadhouse. Alighting would be several ladies of high fashion, disdainfully objecting to the dust of rugged Montana, only to find an oasis of fun and frivolity within the Inn. There would be lavish rooms with an abundance of soap and hot water, luxurious white fluffy towels and large four-poster beds awaiting their arrival. There might be a stray cowpoke or two occupying the single rooms with a shared bath. Just imagine. Then go see for yourself.

Host: Gary Hastings
Address and Contact Numbers:
602 Three Eagle Lane, Big Fork,
MT 59911,
1-406-837-4250
e-mail: coyote@cyberport.net

Somers, Montana

Two favorite bed and breakfast homes are found in Somers, Montana. They are the Osprey Inn and the Outlook Inn. Somers is historically significant for its logging industry. James J. Hill established a mill to make the ties for the Great Northern Railway. Plentiful fir and larch timbers were perfect for ties. The plant to treat the timbers was operational from 1901 until 1986. In early logging days, an eight-foot wooden fence enclosed Somers to keep it a "dry" town. It was playfully nicknamed "Sobers." An early legislative mandate prohibited liquor sales or consumption within five miles of any Montana sawmill.

Osprey Inn

The mascot of the **Osprey Inn Bed and Breakfast** is a bird of prey common to the rivers and lakes of Montana. If you raft or canoe by a dead cottonwood draped with what appears to be a large mop in the topmost branches, you will know you are in the environs of a pair of nesting osprey. A shriek, a plunge and a glint of sunlight on bronze tailfeathers

are all you see of this fisherbird. He retrieves his catch with only droplets of water on his white undercoat.

Wayne and Sharon Finney, who own the Osprey Inn, are avid bird watchers and entertain Audubon enthusiasts from all over the world. The home fronts on beautiful Flathead Lake and offers large comfortable rooms with private baths. Illustrating the Osprey's important feature, is the story about the "Kind-Hearted Woman". . . and man. In yesteryear when hobos were part of the American experience, they had a vocabulary of "hobo signs." One sign, that of a smiling cat, would be chalked or scratched into a fencepost or along the street in front of a house. The smiling cat indicated the presence of a lady of the house who could be counted on for a friendly word, a blessing or even a warm meal. The Finney home is a house of the smiling cat. This strata is part of their Kind-Hearted repertoire.

Osprey Inn's Morning Strata

2 cups shredded thawed hash browns
1 dozen eggs
½ cup sour cream
2 cups chopped cooked ham
½ cup diced green pepper
¼ cup diced scallions
1 cup sliced zucchini
1 cup sliced mushrooms
1 teaspoon crushed herbs i.e., dill, rosemary, basil, lemon pepper and thyme
2 cups shredded cheddar cheese

Slather 9x13-inch baking dish with butter. Spread thawed hash browns over bottom. Layer ham, peppers, scallions, zucchini and mushrooms over potatoes. In a separate bowl, beat eggs; add sour cream, add herbs and mix. Pour egg mixture over layered ingredients. Sprinkle with cheese. Bake 1 hour at 350°F. Cool for 10 minutes, serve with salsa.

Host and Hostess: Wayne and Sharon Finney
Address and Contact Numbers:
5557 Highway 93 South, Somers, MT 59932
1-800-258-2042, 1-406-857-2042
www.ospreybnb.com

Outlook Inn

Todd Ahern and Michelle McGovern built the **Outlook Inn Bed and Breakfast** home. They especially enjoy children and will provide nanny services if necessary. Outlook Inn stands high above Somers where Michelle's

family have homesteaded and been a part of the Swan Valley for almost a century. As in the spirit of the old-fashioned barn raising, neighbors proudly contributed to the completion of this home. Pine logs from the exposed ceiling beams to the baseboards make up the timber construction.

The four guestrooms with queen beds and private baths have separate themes celebrating the life around Flathead Lake. For instance, the "Native Son" has cathedral ceilings that accentuate the golden sponge painting and pictograph-like art of the Native Americans. The wall of the great room displays a bear that was bagged on Boon Road just below the Outlook. A river rock fireplace enhances another wall and a large hand-hewn table provides room for everyone to congregate and swap stories while they enjoy a fresh cup of gourmet coffee and croissants with fresh huckleberry syrup.

Outlook Inn Croissants

12 croissants
8 eggs
1 tablespoon orange rind
Dollop of milk
Scant teaspoon of vanilla

Beat eggs, orange rind, milk and vanilla together in a pie dish. Cut croissants in half. Preheat griddle and grease with melted butter or pan spray. Dip croissant halves in batter and fry on both sides until golden brown and serve with huckleberry syrup. Serves 8.

Outlook Inn Granola

6 cups of oatmeal
1 cup each: raw sunflower seeds, slivered almonds, powdered milk,
 coconut and wheat germ
½ cup oil
1 cup honey

In a largs bowl mix dry ingredients. In sauce pan heat oil and honey, to runny consistency but do not boil. Pour honey mixture over dry ingredients and mix well. Spread on a large cookie sheet. Bake at 300°F for one hour or until brown. Stir occasionally to keep from burning.

Host and Hostess: Todd Ahern and Michelle McGovern
Address and Contact Numbers:
175 Boon Road, Somers, MT 59932
1-888-857-8439, 1-406-857-2060
www.webby.com/montana/outlook
e-mail: outlook@digisys.net

Keith House

Step back in history and recreate a family heritage with skill and elegance. Step back in time and give a vintage home the comforts of a new century. A love of heritage and a flair for interior design make the **Keith House Mansion Bed and Breakfast** standout among bed and breakfast homes.

The Keith House Mansion honors the Keith Family. They were among Kalispell's first successful business people. The railroads and mercantiles were ripe for the management skills of Harry Keith. He supplied merchants and residents with the goods they needed to prosper in a booming frontier community. This golden age of Kalispell lasted from the end of the nineteenth century until after World War I. The Keith House was built, occupied and maintained by the Keiths for most of that era.

An afternoon is easily squandered at this Queen Anne style bed and breakfast home. Spacious, yet cozy, the main floor is designed to attract your eye from one elegant detail to the next. In the living room, roebuck in red tiled bas-relief highlight the fireplace. The wreath stencil of red and green ivy remind one of a Christmas theme that is tastefully replayed in every corner of the mansion using tartan plaids, Laura Ashley florals and Battenburg lace. If the weather turns cool or you

need to relax after a day of skiing, the library, with its intimate fireplace, is a perfect place to curl up with a good book.

A commanding staircase in the middle of the foyer invites the new arrival to a second

story area of guestrooms with
queen beds and private baths.
Upstairs and down, the work
of Russell Chatam, Monte
Dolack and Linda Tippetts is
enjoyed.

Each morning the kitchen
comes alive with preparations
for good cooking like the fol-
lowing recipes. Near the dining room ceiling, around the perimeter of
the room, is an inspiring message in calligraphy by Karen Leigh. The
Word from Hebrews 13:2 reads, "Do Not Forget To Entertain Strangers, For Thereby Some Have Entertained Angels Unaware."

Basil Grilled Chicken

¾ teaspoon ground pepper
4 chicken breast halves, skinned
¼ cup butter
¼ cup fresh basil, chopped
½ cup butter softened
2 tablespoons grated Parmesan cheese
¼ teaspoon garlic powder
1/8 teaspoon salt
1/8 teaspoon pepper
fresh basil sprigs

Press ¾ teaspoon of pepper into meaty sides of chicken. Combine ¼
cup melted butter and ¼ cup chopped basil; stir well. Brush chicken
lightly with melted butter mixture. Combine ½ cup soft butter, 2 teaspoons basil, Parmesan cheese, garlic, salt and pepper in a small bowl.
Beat at low speed with electric mixer until smooth and well blended.
Grill chicken over medium coals 8-10 minutes on each side, basting
frequently. Serve grilled chicken with basil-butter mixture. Garnish
with fresh basil sprigs. Serves 4.

The Keith House Asparagus Frittata

1 tablespoon olive oil
1 clove garlic, minced
4 shallots, minced
1 red pepper julienned
¾ pound asparagus, tough ends discarded, cut into 1½-inch pieces, steamed until bright green, reserve 8 tips
7 eggs
1½ cups grated Swiss or Provolone cheese
salt, pepper, chervil to taste
½ cup fine French bread crumbs
¼ cup grated Parmesan cheese

Preheat oven to 350°F. Generously grease 9x13-inch baking pan. In a small sauté pan, heat olive oil over medium high heat. Add garlic, shallots and red pepper. Stir-fry for 4 minutes. Mix into asparagus and spread evenly over bottom of baking dish. In medium mixing bowl, beat eggs with cheese and spices. Pour over asparagus, sprinkle top with breadcrumbs, then Parmesan. Cover tightly with aluminum foil. Bake at 350°F for 25 minutes. Remove foil and bake another 20 minutes or until browned and knife inserted in center comes out clean. Cut into 8 pieces and garnish each serving with asparagus tip.

Host and Hostess: Dan and Rebecca Bauder
Address and Contact Numbers:
538 5th Avenue East, Kalispell, MT 59901
1-800-972-7913, 1-406-752-7933
e-mail: keithbb@digisy.net

Conrad Mansion

The Conrad Mansion is not a bed and breakfast; rather it was the home of C. E. Conrad who is called "Montana pioneer, Missouri River trader, freighter and founder of the city of Kalispell." The Conrad Mansion with its Tiffany glass windows and its untouched detail is on the National Register of Historic Places. It is within walking distance of Woodland Park and forty minutes driving distance from Glacier Park.

Address and Contact Numbers:
P.O. Box 1041, Kalispell, MT 59903
1-406-755-2166

Stillwater Inn

Before you leave the community of Kalispell, there is another home in the historic district called **Stillwater Inn Bed and Breakfast**. The Stillwater is restored to its former grandeur. It boasts mission oak detail and stained glass windows. The Raised Waffles are unique for their combination of baking powder and yeast.

Raised Waffles

½ cup warm water
1 packet dry yeast
2 cups milk
½ cup melted margarine or butter
1 teaspoon salt
1 tablespoon sugar
2 cups flour
2 eggs
¼ teaspoon baking powder
rind of 1 orange
2 tablespoons Grand Marnier
1 teaspoon fresh grated or ground nutmeg

In a large mixing bowl sprinkle water with dry yeast. Let stand 5 minutes. Add milk, butter, salt, sugar and flour to yeast. Mix until smooth. Cover with plastic and let stand overnight at room temperature. In the morning, beat in eggs, soda, orange rind and Grand Marnier. Stir until well mixed; batter will be thin.

Pour into waffle pan and bake until golden and crisp.

Host and Hostess: Ray and Kathy Dockter
Address and Contact Numbers:
206 4th Avenue East, Kalispell, MT 59901
1-800-398-7024, 1-406-755-7080
e-mail: psalm23@in-tch.com

Creston Country Inn

The **Creston Country Inn Bed and Breakfast** lets travelers know

there is still prairie land in the Flathead Valley where you can see unfettered views of Glacier Park. The Creston is a solid restored farmhouse on twenty-five acres of rich farmland. The flowers surrounding this country home bloom in profusion all spring, sum-

mer and fall. The four guestrooms are Valley Vista, Mount View, Sunrise and Canterbury.

The owners, Rick and Ginger, are a nurse and teacher team. Their well-appointed dining and guest area can accommodate about eight people for breakfast. Guests can explore the farmlands and wander along the creek or easily hike in Glacier Park and return to the Creston for the night. This egg puff is Ginger's favorite and she cooks it on a country cookstove. Attention is paid to cleanliness. Individual servings of the egg puff and an accompanying muffin or breakfast roll allow transfer without touching.

Creston Egg Puff

8 large eggs
½ cup milk
1 cup grated cheese

1½ cup Canadian bacon, chopped
½ teaspoon dried or fresh basil
¼ teaspoon white pepper
¼ teaspoon salt
1 English muffin crumbled in blender

Preheat oven to 350°F. Butter or spray 4-5 8-ounce ramekins. Whisk eggs and milk together; add all other ingredients. Bake 30-35 minutes, until puffed, golden and firm. Serve with basil sprig or salsa. Serves 4.

Host and Hostess: Rick Malloch and Ginger Lockner
Address and Contact Numbers:
70 Creston Road, Kalispell, MT 59901
1-800-257-7517, 1-406-755-7517
www.wtp.net/go/crestoninn

Plum Creek Bed and Breakfast

Your hostess Caroline operates Flathead Valley's long-established bed and breakfast home on the banks of Plum Creek. The ranch-style **Plum Creek House Bed and Breakfast** has a common area that over-hangs Glacier Park's Flathead River. The area is accessible by Amtrak rail, and Delta and Horizon flights into Glacier International Airport.

The historical significance of Plum Creek, originally built by D. C. Dunham in 1957, is tied to the timber company of the same name. Dunham began his timber business in Bemidji, Minnesota. When un-favorable conditions prevailed, he was forced to look for other places to reestablish his company. Dunham moved his operation, employees and all, to Columbia Falls in 1946. Plum Creek is an operational tim-ber company.

The bed and breakfast guest areas overlook the river and Glacier Park. Various ameni-ties include a sunroom, hot tub, heated swimming pool, dining room and a living room with a telescope to view wild-life. Bear, coyote, otter, eagle, osprey, deer, elk, wolf, ducks, geese and a variety of other birds live along the riverbanks and thicket below the Plum Creek House. Guest areas with private baths and a full country breakfast make this bed and breakfast very easy to use for an entire vacation.

Western Breakfast Casserole

6-8 tortillas
4-5 cups Mexicheese or cheddar
2-3 cups parboiled broccoli
8-10 slices ham or 4 cups cooked sausage
½ cup mushrooms
½ cup onions
16 eggs
1 cup milk
lemon pepper to taste

Slather sides and bottom of 9x13-inch pan with melted margarine. Layer tortillas to cover sides and bottom. Sprinkle 1 cup grated cheese over

tortillas. Layer broccoli, ham (or sausage), mushrooms and onions to cover pan; sprinkle with lemon pepper. Mix in separate bowl eggs, milk, remaining 4 cups of cheese and salt; pour over meat and vegetables. Bake at 350°F for 45 minutes or until knife inserted in middle comes out clean. Allow to cool and set for 15 minutes. Slice and serve with salsa or hot sauce. Serves 6-8.

Deluxe Chicken Casserole

4 cups cooked, diced chicken
8 teaspoons finely chopped onion
2 cups chopped walnuts
6 cups cooked rice
4 cans cream of chicken soup
2 teaspoons salt
4 cups diced celery
2 teaspoons pepper
4 tablespoons lemon juice
3¾ cup mayonnaise
1 cup water
6 cups crushed potato chips.

In a large bowl or stockpot, mix all ingredients except mayonnaise, water, eggs and potato chips. Combine water and mayonnaise and add to other ingredients. Top with potato chips and bake at 400ºF or until casserole bubbles. Serves 20. Popular for luncheons. A variation of this includes diced green and red bell pepper, carrots and cooked wild rice for color. A turkey roaster pan can be used for this casserole. The potato chips are added the last ten minutes of cooking time so they brown without becoming soggy.

Hostess: Caroline Stevens
Address and Contact Numbers:
985 Vans Avenue, Columbia Falls, MT 59912
1-800-682-1429, 1-406-892-1816
www.wtp.net/go/plumcreek
e-mail: plumcreek@in-tch.com

Gasthaüs Wendlingen

Gasthaüs Wendlingen Bed and Breakfast provides the best of American-German food and tradition. "Zimmer Frei" on the door is a welcome sight to people who have visited bed and breakfast homes in Germany. It has the

pleasant ring of, "our home is ready for guests." Gasthaüs Wendlingen is located in a valley of daisies and woodlands near Whitefish within sight of the Big Mountain ski area.

Eight acres for hiking and enjoying the woodlands include a trail that overlooks Haskill Creek and a beaver dam. The Küegler Zimmer overlooks these meadows. The room name honors Hedel Küegler who emigrated from Germany to New York in 1935. Other rooms have names that relate to the family heritage. The Wendlingen home is named after an ancestral town in Germany where the grandpa or *opa* lived. All rooms have queen, king or twin beds. Other creature comforts include a steam sauna that makes relaxation available after a day of skiing, golfing or hiking.

The Gasthaüs Wendlingen has two guest entries. The large Western-style porch is attached to the great room and its rock fireplace and sitting area. The front porch is off the dining area and kitchen where

you can fill up on German *schpatzle* (noodles) with *lieberkässe* (veal) or poached *lochs* (salmon) with German potato salad. Barb creates a variety of ethnic breads and strudel. Here is a favorite cake.

German Crumb Cake

1 cup sugar
2 cups flour
¼ pound butter or margarine
2 teaspoon baking powder
2 eggs
½ teaspoon salt
¼ cup milk
1 teaspoon vanilla

Preheat oven to 350ºF. Mix sugar, butter, eggs, salt, flour and milk. Add more milk, a little at a time if cake batter is too thick. Pour into greased 9x13-inch pan.

Crumb topping:
1 cup sugar
2½ cups sifted flour
½ pound cold butter
Mix flour and sugar, then dice cold butter into mixture. Consistency must be firm and moist. Topping should hold together in pea-sized particles. Sprinkle crumb topping over cake batter. Bake at 350ºF for 30-35 minutes or until golden brown.

Host and Hostess: Bill and Barbara Klein

Address and Contact Numbers:
700 Monegan Road, Whitefish,
MT 59937
1-800-811-8002, 1-406-862-4886

Location:
At the junction of Highway 93 and
Highway 40, take 40 2.3 miles
toward Glacier Park to Dillon Rd.
Go 1 mile to Monegan Road and
turn left on Monegan Road. Go 1
mile.

Schiefelbein Haus

The Schiefelbein Haus on Flathead Lake serves "a bit of Bavaria" to folks traveling and residing in Glacier Country. During the summer, you can eat in the sun or shade of the outdoor Beer Garden. On the menu are brautworst, sauerkraut, wiener schnitzel, schapzel and German potato salad plus a variety of Bavarian desserts, breads and German and American brews. All entrees are delicious home-cooked fare.

German Potato Salad

6 medium potatoes
2 tablespoons bacon drippings or butter
¼ cup finely chopped scallions
½ cup rice vinegar
1 teaspoon sugar
½ teaspoon salt
¼ teaspoon paprika
¼ teaspoon dry mustard

Boil potatoes with jackets until tender. Peel and cube into ½ inch pieces. Melt butter and sauté scallions. Add potatoes turning until golden brown.
Bring to boil vinegar, sugar and spices, mixing thoroughly. Pour over potatoes and combine. Sprinkle with fresh or dried parsley or chives.

Host and Hostess: Stephen and Darlene Schiefelbein
Address and Contact Numbers:
6395 East Shore, Highway 35, Polson, MT 59860
1-406-887-2431

Huckleberry Hannah's

Huckleberry Hannah's Bed and Breakfast is located in the northwestern corner of Montana on the high plains of Tobacco Valley. This valley, four miles south of the Canadian border, boasts 180 frost-free days a year. The Kootenai found the growing season favorable for the tobacco used in their ceremonial peace pipes.

Huckleberry Hannah (Deanna Doying-Hansen) and her husband, Jack, have put their talents and personalities into this log inn. Dracena, friendship ivy and jade frame the sunny window areas and reflect the surrounding greenery that borders the lake.

The guest areas accommodate twenty-five people. A dining area that opens to a deck adjoins a kitchen where Huckleberry Hannah creates her country cookbooks. The clever incorporation of recipes and story line shares the old-fashioned correspondence of Hannah and her friend Emily. The letters tell the story of the woman who left her kith and kin to settle the West. The present-day Huckleberry Hannah shares a recipe from her second cookbook that is special to Montana appetites.

Orange Quail and Wild Rice

4 whole quail dressed with juice of one orange
½ teaspoon garlic powder
½ teaspoon onion powder
1 teaspoon each, rosemary
thyme, salt and pepper
1 tablespoon melted butter
2 cups white rice, cooked
2 cups wild rice, cooked
1 garlic clove, crushed
1 teaspoon orange zest
¼ teaspoon salt
pinch of parsley

Toss white and wild rice with
orange zest, crushed garlic, ½ teaspoon salt, and parsley. In a small
bowl mix juice and remaining seasonings. Baste birds with juice mixtures. Stuff birds with rice mixture and place in roaster. Bake at 350°F
for 30 minutes, turning once and basting one more time with juice.
Baste with half the melted butter and continue roasting for 15 minutes.
Note: When quail are not in season, this recipe works for Cornish game
hens. Reduce thyme, rosemary, salt and pepper to ½ teaspoon each.

Host and Hostess: Jack and Deanna Doying
Address and Contact Numbers:
3100 Sophie Lake Road, Eureka, MT 59917
1-888-889-3381, 1-406-889-3381
Location:
At north end of Eureka turn left on highway 37, go 1 mile, turn right on Airport
Road, go 3 miles. Turn left on Tetrault Lake Road, go 2 miles. Turn left on Sophie
Lake Road, go 700 feet and follow drive of Hannah's.

A Wild Rose

A Wild Rose Bed and Breakfast is an elegant home for all seasons.
The deep rose of summer is
dappled by the changing
leaves of fall aspen. The white
blanket of winter melts into
vivid green foliage of early
spring. The food and carefully
appointed elegance of A Wild
Rose make it a place to celebrate wedding anniversaries,
Valentine's Day, Christmas
and the Fourth of July.

Brenda and Joseph are veteran trekkers. During college and their adult

careers they have lived and
worked in over thirty-five national parks. Brenda and Joseph could not live without the
wilderness and have accurate
information about Glacier
Park and its network of roads
and trails.

Brenda's lapidary interests
find expression in the Italian and Montana tile and marble accents
throughout A Wild Rose. The luxury continues in the availability of
the spa and its therapeutic
massage. Executive interests
are served, not only in one of
the four rooms with private
baths, but at the information
center and library that guests
use to send and receive fax,
phone, internet, multimedia
and written information.

Spinach Ricotta Lasagna Swirls

8 lasagna noodles
4 cloves roasted garlic, minced
1 10-ounce package frozen chopped spinach, thawed and well drained
2 cups ricotta cheese
1 teaspoon of vegetable salt seasoning or salt
1 cup shredded mozzarella
1 jar of your favorite marinara sauce
parsley sprigs or any fresh herb for garnish

Prepare lasagna noodles as package directs, drain and lay them flat. Combine spinach, ricotta, salt, garlic and most of the mozzarella. Spread each cooked lasagna noodle with a heaping 1/4 cup of mixture. Roll up firmly, jelly-roll fashion. Pour marinara sauce into 12 inch skillet, place rolls seam side down in skillet. Bring to simmer, then reduce heat to low and cook, covered, for about 15 minutes. Top each roll with a little sauce and a sprinkle of remaining mozzarella. Cover and simmer about 5 minutes longer until rolls are heated through. Garnish with fresh herbs. Recipe makes 4 generous servings.

Host and Hostess: Joseph and Brenda Mihalko
Address and Contact Numbers:
10280 Highway 2 East, Coram,
MT 59913
1-406-387-4900
www.cyberport.net/wildrose
e-mail: wildrose@cyberport.net

Mountain Timbers

The majestic timbers of this mountain retreat blend with Glacier's snow-capped peaks. A meadow of daisies is the only visual separation between **Mountain Timbers Bed and Breakfast** and the park.

The Timbers, owned by Dan and June Diamond, is named for the massive four hundred and fifty-year-old larch beams that support its five thousand square feet of living space. Rooms and suites in two wings

of the house accommodate sixteen guests. The common areas are so simply decorated that it is easy to commit detail to memory. Fireplaces, leather couches and an easy chair, floor to ceiling windows, a 1923 Steinway and Native American art dominate the living room.

The pristine character of this home continues in the second floor rooms that are tucked beyond the chalet-style balcony overlooking the living room fireplace. From this vantage point, you continue to see the peaks of Glacier Park. Mandy nods a signal to come and enjoy a delicious break-fast. An urn holds freshly brewed coffee and guests serve themselves and join the friendly chatter around the long plank table. The trout for breakfast is prepared with ba-con and garnished with al-monds.

Trout Amandine

Fry several slices of bacon in a skillet on medium heat. When browned, turn over. Place gutted and cleaned trout butterfly-style over bacon and fry until cooked and flaky. Remove trout and bacon. Fry ½ cup almonds in bacon grease until crisp. Drain al-monds and set aside leaving 2

tablespoons of bacon drippings in pan. Replace trout in hot pan, frying on each side until flaky. Remove trout from pan and season to taste with salt and pepper. Top with almonds and garnish with fresh greens and lemon slices.

Hostess: Mandy Joubert
Address and Contact Numbers:
Box 127, West Glacier, MT 59936
1-800-841-3835, 1-406-387-5830
By Reservation Only

Paola Creek

"Feeling at home in a timber palace," describes a stay at **Paola Creek Bed and Breakfast**. The owners, Kelly and Les, milled, peeled and secured the timber construction of their home. Through the main window, you see the cap and beard of Glacier Park's

famous St. Nicholas Peak. From any of the four guestrooms, you view the inviting common area that sports large couches around a fireplace that can be fired up any time of the year. Each room is clean and simple with a private bath and a queen bed covered with a hand-made quilt. Beyond the living room you can gaze to the mountains or to the kitchen where preparations for all meals of the day are in progress.

Unique touches include a commercial kitchen because Paola Creek is in the wilderness. Kelly prepares lunches for hikers who book stays for one to two weeks. Dinners are offered by reservation. Paola Creek is sweetly scented with herbs from gardens inside and outside the house. There is a greenhouse garden adjacent to the kitchen. The door holds a hanging herb bouquet where rosemary, oregano and thyme are handy. Outside gardens are planted with annuals when the snow melts.

Host and Hostess: Kelly and Les Hostetler

Address and Contact Numbers:
HC 36, Box 4C, Essex, MT 59916
1-888-311-5061, 1-406-888-5061
www.wtp.net/go/paola
e-mail: paola@in-tch.com
Location:
Mile marker 172.8 on Highway 2
East

Aspenwood

Aspenwood Bed and Breakfast is on the northern plains of Montana beyond the eastern border of Glacier Park. It gets its name from the aspen and willow in the coulee of the Milk River. Pat Smith is owner and chef of the

Aspenwood. Her commercial partners are Larry Ground and Robert Black Bull. In the main lodge are three bedrooms with private baths.

Or you could sleep in one of the teepees on the summer campgrounds near the lodge.

Tantamount to the Aspenwood's beds and cuisine is the calendar of events for the summer months. Aspenwood's partners are active in the lives of Native American youth from the Browning area. The International Traditional Games and the Blackfeet Buffalo Horse Ranch are two new ventures supported by the Aspenwood.

Cuisine for summer events will include cooking by chefs-in-residence from Poland, Ecuador and the southern United States. In addition to meals and relaxation, Pat, an acrylic artist, offers workshops to her guests and area residents.Pat shares this dinner recipe from the Aspenwood.

Easy Chicken Pot Pie

¾ cup frozen mixed vegetables
1 cup cooked and diced chicken
1 can condensed cream of mushroom soup
1 cup of dry Bisquick baking mix
½ cup milk
1 large egg

Preheat oven to 400°F. Mix vegetables, chicken and soup and pour in greased 9-inch pie pan. Mix Bisquick, milk and egg with fork until blended. Spread over chicken and vegetable mix. Bake 30 minutes or until golden brown. Serves 6.

Hostess: Pat Smith
Address and Contact Numbers:
Box 1763, Browning, MT 59417
1-800-775-1355, 1-406-338-7911

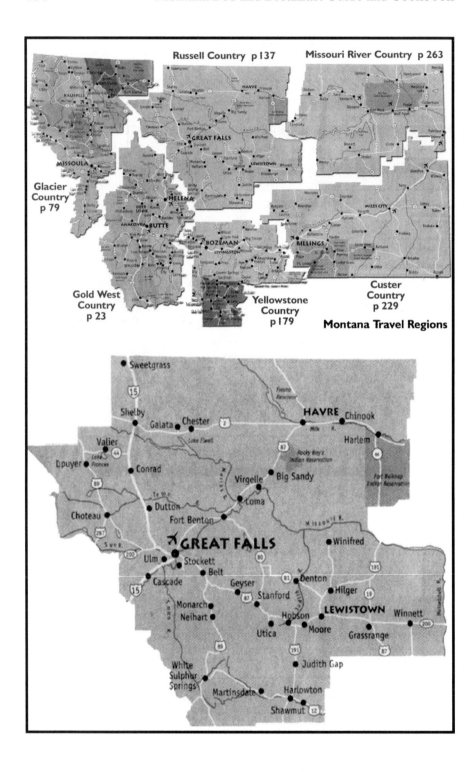

Russell Country p 137

Missouri River Country p 263

Glacier
Country
p 79

Gold West
Country
p 23

Yellowstone
Country
p 179

Custer
Country
p 229

Montana Travel Regions

Charlie Russell Country

Laugh Kills Lonesome

He called it *Laugh Kills Lonesome*.
Shows old friends around the fire
An' them boys is swappin' windys
Long before they savvied wire.

Charlie stands there in the firelight.
He's the nighthawk who's rode in.
He, mostly, talked to hosses.
Sang nightsongs to the wind.

That paintin' shows another time
When man rode all alone
An' yarning by the cookfire
Made a wagon seem like home.

You can feel ol' Charlie mournin'
He'd 'a give up wealth an' fame
To ride back down them old trails
Before the land was tame.

Laugh Kills Lonesome, Charlie loved it,
That time now long ago,
When the wind still blew, unfettered,
From the Milk to Mexico.

Cowboy Poet, Mike Logan

The abrupt change in scenery as you leave the snow-capped peaks of Glacier Country and enter Charlie Russell Country is deceptive. The eye travels over expanses of grassland, but look more closely and appreciate the subtle beauty of the Rocky Mountain Front. Nearly twenty thousand acres of foothills called Pine Butte Swamp are part of the Nature Conservancy. Eons ago, rich plant life supported the survival of dinosaurs. Attesting to their history are bones, eggs and the trace of rookeries that belonged to the "lizard-birds" of Egg Mountain. The Museum of the Rockies in Bozeman documents these dinosaurs and other paleontology of Montana. The museum hosts a traveling exhibit of life-sized replicas that snort and move to give visitors a lifelike experience that help envision life at Egg Mountain.

As the mountains fade into the distance, the prairie tablelands put you on top of the world. There is a reason Montana feels like Big Sky Country and the intensity of that feeling increases on these remote plains. Native American Blackfeet knew this part of Montana as their hunting ground. Vast herds of buffalo roamed as far as the eye could see. An historical marker south of Dupuyer creaks on its hinges as gusts of prairie wind rock it to and fro. Someone has written:

Blackfeet and Buffalo

In the days of fur traders and trappers, immediately following the time of the Lewis and Clark expedition, notably 1804-06, all of this country bordering the Rocky Mountains north to Canada and south to the Three Forks of the Missouri and to the Yellowstone River was buffalo range and hunting ground of the Blackfeet Nation. These Indians fiercely guarded their territory from invasion. Like all of the Plains Indians, they were dependent upon the buffalo for their existence. The herds meant meat, moccasins, robes, leggings and teepees - board and room on the hoof. Some Indian legends say that the first buffalo came out of a hole in the ground. When the seemingly impossible happened and the buffalo were wiped out, there were Indians who claimed that Whites found the spot, hazed the herds back into it, and plugged the hole.

Inn Dupuyer

There is a beautiful oasis in the desert of bunch grass. It is called **Inn Dupuyer Bed and Breakfast**. Rita and Joe Christiaens appreciate Charlie Russell, the painter whom Russell Country commemorates. They know the country that Russell captured in his paintings. For example, Russell's painting, *Jerkline*, depicts the kind of freighter that brought Rita's great-grandmother to the Dupuyer area. Freighters were the a brand of men who dared to cross the hunting grounds described in "Blackfeet and Buffalo." Their cargo was a bulky assortment of mining supplies, household furnishings and dry goods for mercantile centers. Sometimes the cargo was "people" who hitched a ride hoping to reach a central point in the West. Perhaps they carried a frayed letter in their pocket affirming the whereabouts of a certain family member, or maybe hard luck drove them far from home to brighter promises in the West. Whatever their situation, they were energized by the prospects at the end of their journey.

Freighters traveled together for protection. The purpose of their bold adventure was to make money crossing unsettled territory. Stopping at a central location, the freighter unloaded his cargo to slower pack horses or mule trains. Rita's great-grandmother and her two teenage daughters started with a freighter in Omaha, Nebraska. That leg of the journey ended in Helena, Montana. From there she made her way north and settled in the Dupuyer area.

It is appropriate that the Christiaens be ambassadors for Russell Country. Both Rita and Joe grew up around Dupuyer and their inn is like a museum for those who are proud of their pioneer heritage. When people

heard about the Christiaens' plans for a bed and breakfast, they donated antiques, retold family stories and contributed pictures to validate the history of Inn Dupuyer and Pondera County.

The Christiaens capture the essence of the country within the inn. The hand-hewn log homestead is over a century old. It was built before Dupuyer was a platted town site. Joe and Rita have added four bedrooms and private baths with care not to destroy the homogeneity of an historical landmark. There are traces of frontier elegance in a bedroom that is complete with a splendid white coverlet, a marble statuette, high-backed chairs, a small chandelier and a gold-fringed carpet over a refurbished pine floor. Another room with chinked walls, cured hides and rich blankets contains bits of memorabilia from the

long-forgotten beaver trapper. Tales of Native American Blackfeet valor permeate the whitewashed walls of a cozy room on the first floor. This room contains medicine bag and buffalo skull, two totems of the Blackfeet. Sharing breakfast is delightful in a sunny dining area. New ceilings and walls replace the mud chinking which had degenerated beyond rescue.

Host and Hostess: Joe and Rita Christiaens
Address and Contact Numbers:
11 Jones West, Dupuyer, MT 59432
1-406-472-3241

Country Lane

Driving along Highway 89 north of Choteau, a splash of color catches your eye. A plum-red Case tractor pulling a honeywagon loaded with a profusion of petunias bears a sign, **"Country Lane Bed and Breakfast**." This country home is owned and hosted by artist Ann Arensmeyer.

Creativity and elegance are the hallmarks of Country Lane, where you can enjoy an enclosed solar swimming pool and use the gift shop in your spare

moments. Ann sells her paintings of Montana animals, floral bouquets and country scenes. She also carries a variety of brochures about points of interest in Russell Country.

The Country Lane had humble beginnings as an out-building on fifty-eight acres of the Spring Creek Game Reserve. Today it is a split-level cedar guest home with a vaulted ceiling. A window seat in the dining room gives birders a view of the woodlands and meadows of Country Lane. The fireplace, refurbished with polished glacial slate, warms the home in hunting season. There are four pleasant rooms with king or queen beds. Ann's love of the Southwest is apparent in the still life pictures of baked clay pottery, maize and moccasins that brighten the walls.

Country Lane is equidistant to Glacier or Yellowstone Park. It is a perfect stopping place for a day of exploration of the Choteau area. The Pine Butte Swamp, the Nature Conservancy and Egg Mountain of the dinosaurs are accessible places of interest.

Freezer Buns

Dough:
5-6 cups flour
½ cup sugar
1 teaspoon salt
½ teaspoon grated lemon peel
2 packages dry yeast
1 cup margarine
1 ⅓ cups water
2 eggs
confectioner's sugar

In large bowl, thoroughly mix 1½ cups flour, sugar, salt, lemon peel and undissolved yeast; add margarine. Gradually add tap water to blended ingredients and beat 2 minutes with mixer at medium speed. Add eggs and ½ cup flour. Beat at high speed 2 minutes. Add enough flour to make a soft dough. Cover and let dough rest for 20 minutes. Turn onto floured board; divide into 3 equal parts. Roll each piece to an 8-inch square and cut into 8 1-inch strips. Twist each strip and coil into a circle, sealing ends underneath. Place on greased baking sheets, making a wide indentation in the center of each coil, pressing to bottom. Spoon prepared filling (see directions below) into indentation, using about 2 tablespoons cheese filling or 1 tablespoon date-nut filling. Freeze until firm. Transfer to plastic bag for use as needed. Retains flavor up to 4 weeks. When ready to use, let stand at room temperature until fully thawed, about 1½ hours. Let rise until double in bulk, about 45 minutes. Bake at 375°F for 15-20 minutes. Sprinkle with powdered sugar. Makes two dozen rolls.

Cheese Filling:
2 8-ounce packages cream cheese
½ cup sugar
1 tablespoon grated lemon peel
2 egg whites

Blend together cream cheese, sugar and lemon rind. Gradually add egg whites.

Date Filling:
2 cups pitted dates
½ cup water
½ cup chopped walnuts

Bring dates and water to boil. Boil until water is absorbed. Blend in chopped nuts.

Hostess: Ann Arensmeyer
Address and Contact Numbers:
Route 2, Choteau, MT 59422
1-406-466-2816, 1-505-865-4412
Location:
Located at mailbox 28, 1½ miles
north of Choteau on Highway 89

Viewforth

The **Viewforth Bed and Breakfast** is a restful home at the junction of Highway 287 and Highway 408 north of Augusta, Montana. Terese and Keith Blanding are a talented couple who left Montana only to return to its wide-open spaces. Their lifestyle allows time for savoring humble interests like creating a home and sowing a garden. A pasture of sheep and a new llama are witness to Keith's shepherding instincts and his love of animals. He designed and built the country-sized Craftsman Bungalow. Its wood and sage green hues are a subtle contrast to Terese's bright garden.

Terese has tested her management skills. She successfully owned and man-

aged Lavender's Blue, a teahouse in Portland, Oregon. Terese's Montana kitchen garden rises from beds built and fortified with local compost, manure and swamp peat. Fascinating examples of dill that supports swallowtail, lavender that attracts sphinx and marigold that repels pests fortify the ecosystem of the garden. Herbs and plants like echinacea, geranium, mint and rhubarb are useful for the medicinal quality of their leaves, flowers, roots or bark. Many of the flowering plants are house-warming presents from neighbors.

The Viewforth's interior is as geometrically pleasing as the exterior. Square wooden shades of wall sconces glow with soft light. They are fashioned after the Craftsman lamps of the early 1900's. Tile floors are symmetrically eye pleasing. Attention to art and design adds harmony to the guest area.

Persian carpets, textiles and antique wallpaper are simple in a room where windows open to the splendor of the Montana prairie with a backdrop of the Rocky Mountain Front. A pewter pitcher, a bold -striped tablecloth and a cascade of garden flowers trim the luncheon table.

The Viewforth boasts two large main floor rooms with queen beds and private baths. A stencil of square berries and symmetrical leaves exemplifies the work of Charles Bennie McIntosh, an artist of the Craftsman era.

Pineapple Sage Breakfast Sausage

1 pound pure ground pork
1 egg
¾ cup fresh bread crumbs
3 tablespoons of finely minced
pineapple sage
½ teaspoon salt
¼ teaspoon white pepper

Mix all ingredients thoroughly,
form into logs 1 inch in diameter
and 3 inches in length. Brown on all sides on medium heat. Continueuntil thoroughly cooked. Garnish with sprigs of fresh pineapple sage.

Host and Hostess: Keith and Terese Blanding

Address and Contact Numbers:
4600 Highway 287, Fairfield, MT 59436
1-406-467-3884
Location:
Leave Augusta going toward Choteau on Highway 287. Go 7 miles north of Augusta; the Viewforth is at the junction of US Highway 287 with MT Highway 408.

Latigo and Lace

Terese Blanding's art finds a market at Latigo and Lace, Sara Walsh's premier art shop in Augusta, Montana. Calligraphy artistically accentuates a drawing of blackberries in vari-  *ous stages of ripeness. It reads, "A billion blackberries, full of themselves and September sun, all just out of reach." Can you taste them?*

Owner: Sara Walsh

Address and Contact Numbers:
Box 345, 124 Main Street, Augusta, MT 59410
1-406-562-3665

Lewis and Clark Interpretive Center

The city of Great Falls has a strong and direct tie to the Lewis and Clark Expedition. Paris Gibson, the founding father of Great Falls, heard stories of the "portage of Lewis and Clark" as they discovered a series of shallows and falls that were crossed by portaging the pirogues. Gibson wanted to see for himself, so he traveled from Fort Benton and immediately grasped the opportunities offered by the mighty waterway at the present-day site of Great Falls. Gibson and his friend James J. Hill had dreams that turn opportunity into reality. Before long, they bought and platted a town site. The rest is history; you can be a party to it with a visit to the Lewis and Clark Interpretive Center.

Your destination is Giant Springs Park at the edge of the Missouri River. A few blocks upstream is the Interpretive Center. Exhibits show how the men portaged the dugouts. With the real Missouri River flowing right behind them, it leaves little to imagination. On the self-guided tour you can listen to the efforts of Meriweather Lewis as he bargained for horses and feel how the Native American lived in the Mandan earth dwellings.

Great Falls has two bed and breakfast homes. The Interpretive Center is within a long hike from the Old Oak Inn. It is a short drive from the Collins Mansion.

Lewis and Clark Interpretive Center
Address and Contact Numbers:
4201 Giant Springs Road, Great Falls, MT 59403
1-406-727-8733

Collins Mansion

Oak pocket doors open to expand the elegant parlour and dining area of the **Collins Mansion Bed and Breakfast**. Victorian detail and the nuptial suite of this mansion make it a fitting place to celebrate a wedding. The mansion originally stood alone on a knoll overlooking Great Falls. It still stands in snow-white opulence. Today it is surrounded by a pleasant neighborhood and protected by evergreens that are a century old.

The Collins Mansion was built in 1891 and commemorates the life of T. E. and Lavinia Collins. Hard times in County Cork, Ireland, brought young Tim Collins and his family to the United States. The Montana Gold Rush brought Collins to Last Chance Gulch as a young man. Industrial and economic pursuits kept T. E. Collins in Great Falls as a banker and an attorney until his death at the turn of the century.

The Collins Mansion is elegant in every detail with a dining area large enough to cater weddings, luncheons, Christmas parties and gala birthday events. A fine oak staircase beckons you to rest and relaxation after the party is over. There are five spacious

bedrooms with private baths on the second floor. Attention to unique details like the lively floral patterns of linen bed covers or the elegant black and gold quilt on a brass four-poster make the rooms comfortable and eye pleasing.

The crumb muffins come with a full breakfast; the pepper jelly is from the menu for catered events.

Banana Crumb Muffins

Dough:
1½ cups flour
1 teaspoon baking powder
1 teaspoon baking soda
½ teaspoon salt
2 large ripe bananas, mashed
¾ cup sugar
1 egg, slightly beaten
1/3 cup butter, melted

Topping:
1/3 cup packed brown sugar
1 tablespoon flour
1/8 teaspoon ground cinnamon
1 tablespoon cold butter or margarine

Combine the dry ingredients in a large bowl. In another bowl, combine bananas, sugar, egg, and butter and mix thoroughly. Stir into dry ingredients until moistened. Fill greased or paper-lined muffin cups ¾ full. Combine the first three topping ingredients; cut in butter until crumbly. Sprinkle over muffins. Bake at 375°F for 18-20 minutes or until muffins test done. Cool in pan 10 minutes until removing to a wire rack. Make 12 muffins.

Pepper Jelly Appetizer

4 red peppers
4 green peppers
4 jalapeno peppers
1 cup white vinegar
6 cups sugar
8 ounces cream cheese
crackers of choice

Seed all peppers. Put in food processor, and chop using the shredder blade. Use 2 cups of the prepared pulp and juice and add the vinegar and sugar. Bring mixture to a hard boil. Remove from heat and add 2 3-ounce packages of liquid Certo. Pack in ½ pint jars and seal. Open each ½ pint as needed and serve over 8-ounce package of cream cheese. Spread on crackers.

Hostesses: Connie Romaine and Diana Unghire
Address and Contact Numbers:
1003 Second Avenue Northwest, Great Falls, MT 59404
1-877-452-6798, 1-406-452-6798

Old Oak Inn

Built in 1908, the **Old Oak Inn** is part of the original town site of Great Falls. Judy Vance, your hostess, has refurbished her six elegant rooms in summery themes.

A conversation piece that embellishes the wainscot hall of the Oak Staricase is a sampler, "Wrought by Mary Sedgwick, 1836, in Dublin, Ireland 'Be Virtuous If You Would Be Happy.'" Mary was 13 years old.

The Teddy Bear Palace has many dancing bears for little folks. A combination of bath, bedrooms and sitting areas comprise a suite for a family. The secluded third floor Rose Suite is for newlyweds. Two other rooms have their own balconies.

Judy is no stranger to early mornings of hard work. Many times guests awaken to the smell of homemade wheat bread and a cup of tea or coffee. In addition, a repast of Breakfast Delite is part of a full breakfast.

Breakfast Delite

1 pound country-style sausage
1 cup shredded cheese of choice
2 cups cream of mushroom soup or soup of choice

12 eggs
1 large package frozen hashbrowns

Brown sausage. Layer ingredients in a 9x12-inch baking dish; hashbrowns, sausage, cheese. Mix cream soup and eggs. Pour over layered ingredients. Bake at 350°F for 1 hour. This recipe is fun because you can experiment with different meat, soups, and cheeses to find your favorite.

Hostess: Judy Vance
Address and Contact Numbers:
709 Fourth Avenue North, Great Falls, MT 59401
1-888-727-5782, 1-406-727-5782

Bull Market Antiques Mall

An added attraction that complements the historical nature of the bed and breakfast homes of Great Falls is the Bull Market Mall. It is a congregation of booths featuring antiques and collectibles like old-fashioned library tables, Weller and Roseville pottery, secretaries, photos and paintings.

Owners: Don and Tina Jacobson
Address and Contact Numbers:
202 Second Avenue South, Great Falls, MT 59405,
1-406-771-1869, 1-406-761-7643

Long's Landing

North of Great Falls, past the confluence of the Missouri with the Sun River, is the rich breadbasket of Montana. Under the big sky, wheat fields are punctuated by a view of the Missouri if you take diversions from the main highway. There is even a dot in the road called Portage that may retain its name from the time of the Lewis and Clark Expedition.

The river is in full view as you reach Fort Benton and the little home called **Long's Landing Bed and Breakfast**. Fort Benton centers on the river. The levee, only two blocks from Long's Landing, is the main thoroughfare of town. You can occupy yourself on the levee all day. Two statues mark its length. Perhaps nowhere else is there a statue to a dog, but the plague on the Statue to Shep eulogizes the dog who met all daily trains

waiting for his perished master. One day the
old dog, not hearing the train's approach, was
mortally wounded.

Another statue, "Explorer of the Marias,"
inspired the logo used on maps and road
signs to identify the Lewis and Clark Trail. It
shows Meriweather Lewis with his monocu-
lar, scoping the Marias River at its confluence
with the Missouri north of Fort Benton. Wil-
liam Clark looks on and Sacagawea sits at their feet with Pomp in a pa-
poose on her back. Their figures loom larger than life, and their awesome
adventure remains etched in history.

The Benton Belle, a paddle-wheel riverboat,
served Fort Benton as a ferryboat. It is refurbished for two-hour Missouri River tours
during the summer months. Union Station is
under renovation as Fort Benton prepares
for the bicentennial celebration of the Lewis
and Clark Journey.

Long's Landing is a clean and neat home with
three guestrooms. The guest area is very
private. The Levee Room has twin beds and
a shared bath; the Nellie Peck, named for the steam boat era, has a queen
bed and private bath. The Brother Van Room, immortalizing the itinerant
Methodist evangelist, has a queen bed and shared bath. Family members
have contributed some of the art items to the guest area. Sticky buns are a
favorite that Amy Long, your hostess, prepares daily using a bread maker.

Sticky Buns

Dough:
3 teaspoons active dry yeast
2 teaspoons fast-rising yeast
3 tablespoons oil
1 teaspoon salt
3 tablespoons sugar
2 tablespoons dry milk powder
3 cups white bread flour
1¼ cups water

Sticky Sauce:
¼ cup butter
½ cup brown sugar
¼ cup light corn syrup
½ cup chopped walnuts or pecans
Filling:
¼ cup soft butter
1 teaspoon cinnamon

Follow manufacturer's directions for putting ingredients into bread machine. The ingredients for the dough can be combined, placed in the machine at night, and programmed to mix in early morning. Take bread dough from machine and prepare. Prepare sticky sauce and pour into greased 9x13-inch pan. Sprinkle with nuts. Gather dough from machine onto a floured surface; it will be sticky. Roll to 10x16-inch rectangle. Spread with soft butter and sprinkle with cinnamon. Roll jellyroll style and pinch seams together. Slice into 1½ -inch pieces. Place in pan on top of sticky sauce; and allow to double in size (about 1 hour). Bake at 375°F for 20-25 minutes, or until golden brown. Cool for 3 minutes, and invert pan so sauce and nuts are on top of buns.

Hostess: Amy Long
Address and Contact Numbers:
1011 17th Street, Fort Benton, MT 59442
1-406-622-3461

Virgelle Mercantile

Nostalgia stabs the heart at **Virgelle Mercantile Bed and Breakfast**. Of any home, it authentically portrays "the last, best place;" Montanans know it will not last. Virgelle is a combination of the first names of Virgil and Ella Blankenbaker. In about 1912 they founded a town which never had a population over twenty-five. Ranches dot the countryside beyond the sandstone cliffs that surround Virgelle. In the mid-1800's communities sprang up along the Missouri because of the riverboat trade. When rail and dam prevailed over the riverboats, little towns along the Missouri died. Undaunted, Virgil, Ella and their neighbors managed to entice a spur of the Great Northern to serve Virgelle. However,when trucks became the primary means of transporting cargo, the small populace left in Virgelle did not have the power of persuasion with the Department of Transportation and the highway is not near Virgelle.

Don Sorensen has the heart to keep what he lovingly calls "A full service ghost town." He realizes the splendor of an untouched ghost town on a famous bend of the river. Don purchased the town site so it would not know the demise characteristic of most ghost towns. And a town unto itself it is. Don has a bed and breakfast that lets you imagine an elegant home-

steader-riverboat era not duplicated any place in the United States. The upstairs guest area, with its wide pine floors, original casements and embossed metal ceilings is fully restored. Blue Willow dishes, high-backed spindle rockers, embroidered linens and large clawfoot bathtubs are practical and of functional elegance.

The four guestrooms are named after a particular incident or person from the past. The

Watanabi room has a picture of the Japanese Watanabi family who found refuge in Virgelle during World War II. Americans of Japanese heritage were ferreted out of corners of the United States and taken to internment camps. Remote Virgelle was the Watanabi's refuge and their neighbors protected them.

The Chancellor Room is named for the merchant who did much to serve the  homesteaders of Virgelle. The main floor of the home was the original Virgelle Mercantile; the living quarters were upstairs. Today the main floor is an antique store. If a trader has a treasure on consignment or Don has found a particular vintage antique, you may purchase it at this unique mercantile. Imagine taking home your own Blue Willow antiques and having tea and lemon bars as a reminder of your splendid Virgelle vacation stay.

Lemon Bars

1½ cups flour
¾ cup butter
1/3 cup powdered sugar
4 eggs
2 cups sugar
¼ cup flour
1 teaspoon baking powder
¼ cup lemon juice
2 teaspoons grated lemon peel

Mix flour, butter and powdered sugar as if for piecrust. Press into a 9x13-inch pan and bake

15 minutes at 350°F. Meanwhile beat eggs and sugar with mixer for 10 minutes. Sift flour and baking powder, add to eggs and sugar. Gently stir in lemon juice and rind. Pour mixture over hot crust. Bake 25 minutes at 350°F or until set.

Missouri River Canoe Company

*The **Missouri River Canoe Company** operates in combination with the Virgelle Bed and Breakfast. The housing for guests of the canoe company is rustic. There are cabins on the Missouri River. A common heated bathhouse keeps guests clean and happy. They may bring their own food to cook over the campfire or they are welcome to breakfast with the guests at the Virgelle Bed and Breakfast.*

Host: Don Sorensen
Address and Contact Numbers:
Box 50, Virgelle, MT 59460
1-800-426-2926, 1-406-378-3110
www.canoemontana.com
e-mail: canoemontana@usa.net

Raven Crest

Nowhere else on the prairie is there such a guest pastime as Varmint Hunt. The **Raven Crest Bed and Breakfast** hosts a Winchester Club of unique

origins and one of the best catering services west of the Missouri. Varmint hunters book trips to Raven Crest two years in advance. Guests find the beautiful grounds and serene prairie a pleasant part of this working grain ranch.

The personification of the varmint to ranchers and farmers is legend. A varmint often refers to a low-life, a scoundrel, scum of the earth . . . a varmint. Varmints are sneaky. Two of their habits can wipe out farms. First, their burrows run just below the surface of the earth, where plants root and multiply. If a crop is planted, they can annihilate a wheat field by feeding on the roots. The trenches created when varmints burrow and nest are death to farm implements. The ground becomes bumpy and difficult to maintain and the varmint becomes the cussed critter.

The raven that inhabits the prairies around Raven Crest is a natural enemy of the varmint. So are the hunters. The home is of modern construction and large with all the amenities. You can watch storm clouds move in across the prairie, there are

books to enjoy, as well as a video library. A gift shop offers handmade items. Harvest season is the prettiest time of year with its early morning sunrises and sunsets that last into the late evening.

Mealtime starts with hors d'oeuvres such as Toads In A Hole with a soda or a glass of wine. Following this is a main course of Cornish game hens with wild rice and chiles. Fresh homemade bread accompanied by asparagus with Hollandaise sauce and a salad complete the meal. A little later, Christina's Hungarian Love Letters, an ethnic dessert specialty is served for dessert.

Hungarian Love Letters

3 cups flour
1¼ cups butter
2 whole eggs
1 egg yolk
½ cup milk
¾ cup walnuts, coarsely ground
¾ cup sugar
½ cup graham cracker crumbs
1 teaspoon ground cinnamon
½ cup raisins, rinsed and dried
2½ pounds green apples, peeled and shredded.

In a large mixing bowl, place 2 2/3 cup flour, setting aside 1/3 cup for dusting. With pastry blender or fork, cut in butter until mixture forms balls the size of peas. Make a well in the center. Pour in 1 whole egg, 1 egg yolk and milk. With 2 spoons, combine liquid and dry ingredients until well blended. Shape into a ball. Turn dough onto floured board and knead until smooth, about 5 minutes. Form into a loaf, wrap in waxed paper, and chill two hours or overnight. In a small bowl, combine nuts, sugar, cracker crumbs and cinnamon; set aside. On a floured surface, divide dough into 3 equal portions. With a floured rolling pin, roll out 1 portion large enough to line the bottom of an 11x18-inch baking pan. Fit dough into pan and spread 2/3 of nut mixture over dough. Distribute raisins evenly over nut mixture. Repeat the process with second portion of dough and put over layer of nuts. Mix apples with remaining nut mixture and spread over second layer of dough. Roll last portion of dough and fit over apples. Crack the remaining egg in a small bowl, beat well and brush over dough. Let stand, and brush again. Dip fork tines in warm water and pokes tines diagonally from upper left to lower right corner of pastry, scoring surface. Repeat, scoring from upper right to lower left corner to create a pattern of crossed lines. Bake at 350°F for 35 minutes or until golden brown. Remove pan to wire rack to cool for several hours. Cut into small rectangles. Serves 30.

Host and Hostess: David and Christina Kidd

Address and Contact Numbers:
Rural Route One, Big Sandy, MT
59520-9705
1-406-378-3121

Our Home

The breezeway between the two entries of **Our Home Bed and Breakfast** overlooks the Havre Valley from one vantage point and the Bear's Paw Mountains from the other. In the distance is Mt. Baldy, 8000 feet above the high plains of Montana. Havre came into existence as the railroad hub of James J. Hill's Great Northern Railway. Commerce and industry have attracted a substantial population base for a century.

Our Home is just as it sounds. Both host and hostess, Owen and Nancy McDonagh, maintain jobs outside of their home business. However, entertaining people, travel and cooking are suitable hobbies for an innkeeper; they happen to be Nancy's favorite avocations. The McDonaghs cater to business people by honoring state and federal travel discounts. Our Home is a drug and alcohol-free home. Shuttle service to Amtrak and the airport is available. The McDonaghs' degrees are in conservation and criminal justice from Montana State University; Nancy quips with a chuckle, "But we welcome Griz as guests." Breakfast includes a unique, easy recipe called M.J.'s Dutch Babies. Note that the recipe contains no salt or sugar and is acceptable for diabetic diets.

M.J.'s Dutch Babies

¹/₃ cup butter
4 eggs
1 cup milk
1 cup flour

Melt butter in baking pan in oven. Mix eggs in blender on high; add milk. Blend on high; add flour. Pour into a 9x13-inch pan. For metal pan bake at 425°F for 20-25 minutes, or glass pan at 400°F for 20-25 minutes or until puffy. Serve warm with syrup or fruit and whipped cream. They will look like Dutch babies in a blanket.

Host and Hostess: Owen and Nancy McDonagh
Address and Contact Numbers:
66 65th Avenue Northwest, Havre, MT 59501-5700
1-406-265-1055
www.hiline.net/~donagh
e-mail: donagh@hi-line.net

Pheasant Tales

Lewistown, named to honor Meriweather Lewis, is located in central Montana, southeast of Havre. You meander into the hills above Lewistown. Located on a sunny knoll surrounded by wild flowers and several stand of pines is **Pheasant Tales Bed and Bistro**. This modern log fortress provides a variety of vacation memories. There are large meadows for exploring and identifying flora and fauna. Spring Creek can be fished and the meadows and the ambiance of Pheasant Tales are adapted to the bird hunter.

Note that Pheasant Tales is a bistro or restaurant instead of a bed and breakfast. Chris and Rick Taylor offer evening fare in addition to breakfast. The evening meal is provided upon request with an extra charge and a gourmet breakfast is available for eight dollars per person. The price of a room with a private bath includes a continental breakfast. There is also a suite for four family members that has its own kitchen.

The pheasant motif reminds guests of the environment of Pheasant Tales and bird hunting. Chris says of the grouse or French sharptail, "This dish is a tribute to the enjoyment of the hunt."

French Sharptail

breasts of 4 sharptail grouse, reserve heart and liver for paté
½ cup rice flour
½ teaspoon freshly ground pepper
2 tablespoons olive oil
2 tablespoons Madeira wine
four cubes (4 tablespoons) chicken or pheasant demi-glaze
bouquet garni of fresh thyme and rosemary
several dashes of Galiano

Combine rice flour and ground pepper, set aside. Cover grouse breasts with protective layer of plastic; pound breasts gently with meat mallet enough to tenderize. Lightly flour breasts in flour mixture. Heat olive oil in non-stick sauté pan until hot but not smokey. Sear breasts on both sides; do not brown. Remove  meat from pan and set aside. Coat pan with Madeira, add demi-glaze and spices. Add Galiano and bring to simmer. Add breasts and simmer on medium low heat for 15 minutes, turning breasts until they are tender. DO NOT OVERCOOK. Serve with baked saffron rice.

Host and Hostess: Rick and Chris Taylor
Address and Contact Numbers:
Rural Route One, Lewistown, MT 59657
1-406-538-7880
www.tein.net/pheasant
e-mail: rickt@tein.net

Symmes-Wicks House

The back roads to Lewistown take you through fields punctuated only by a square butte or two like Charlie Russell used in his paintings. In fact, the exact one he used is called Square Butte and it is the singular point of reference in the little town by the same name.

The beautiful, historic **Symmes-Wicks House Bed and Breakfast** is found in the heart of Lewistown. Its contrast to Pheasant Tales gives bed and breakfast enthrusiasts a choice of places to stay.

When Lewistown began to grow as a town site in the early 1900's, the expense of Victorian architectural detail was eclipsed by the economy of a simpler bungalow-style home. The railroad versus the riverboat trade had a lot to do with the economy and the availability of attractive, adequate building materials for use by the common Western settler. Catalog companies like Montgomery-Ward were popular and the rail brought every item imaginable to Montana - even part and parcel of a house, with directions for reassembly. The homes were complete with arches, columns and fireplaces. Victorian homes used imported oak and marble for enhancement detail. The bungalow used local products.

The Symmes-Wicks House represents an adaptation of the architectural styles of the early 1900's. The Victorian gambrels are gone, in its place is a wide roof over three stories of beautifully appointed space. Local artisans chiseled the sandstone blocks from a spring creek quarry. The beautifully crafted wood and brickwork in the guest areas add elegant, warm and comfortable detail.

Charles and Carole Wicks have
spent many years bringing this
home back to life. The attention
to guests is expressed in the fun
it can be to serve people a gourmet breakfast on "lovely pale and
fragile stemware." And there is

an abundance of stories to tell as Charles and Carole have a versatile lifestyle,
love to travel and enjoy meeting people from every part of the world. Carole's

artistic talents are noticeable in
items like the floor cloth that became a quality wall hanging. Or
the choice of Laura Ashley sweet
pea and trellis in a room flooded
with the light from four large windows. Foods like this Tomato,
Cheese, Herb Tart are served
with colorful fruit and garnishes.

Tomato, Cheese, Herb Tart

Crust:
1¼ cup flour
¼ teaspoon salt
½ cup chilled butter, into pieces
4 tablespoons ice water

Combine all ingredients in food processor until reaching the consistency of
coarse meal. Add water to form moist ball and wrap in plastic. Refrigerate
for 35 minutes. Roll out dough; place in 12-inch tart pan. Bake at 350ºF for
15 minutes. Line with foil and layer with dry beans. Dry beans are for
holding foil. Remove foil and beans and bake for 15 minutes more. Cool
on rack. Can set for as long as one day. Cover, keep at room temperature.

Filling:
4-8 tomatoes peeled and cut into ½ inch slices, allow to drain
8 ounces Emmenthal or Gruyere cheese
1 tablespoon fresh basil, or
1 teaspoon dried basil
1 teaspoon fresh thyme
3 tablespoons Parmesan cheese
pepper

Place Emmenthal or Gruyere cheese on baked crust. Arrange Parmesan cheese over tomatoes. Sprinkle herbs over tomatoes. Season with pepper. Bakeat 375°F for 15 minutes, or until cheese melts. Cool slightly. Remove sides of tart pan. Cut into wedges and serve. Makes 12 -15 appetizers.

Host and Hostess: Charles and Carole Wicks
Address and Contact Numbers:
220 West Boulevard, Lewistown, MT 59457
1-406-538-9068

Valley of Peace

Historical accounts of the Native American Blackfeet Nation describe a "Valley of Peace" where weary warriors carried their battle-scarred brothers to a warm sulphur springs for healing. Today as you enter White Sulphur Springs from any direction the peace of that long-past time is still on the wind. Out on the prairie nestled among the hills of the Castle and Belt mountain ranges are two delightful bed and breakfast homes called Montana Mountain Lodge and Skylodge.

Montana Mountain Lodge

Montana Mountain Lodge Bed and Breakfast is located on Scenic Route 89 southeast of Great Falls. It is minutes from the Showdown Ski Resort and steps away from two hundred miles of groomed snowmobile trails. The lodge is boundaried on three sides by the Lewis and Clark National Forest. It overlooks Sheep Creek where you can literally "fish from the front yard" or dream in your easy chair about the big one that got away.

Jean Cooney Roberts grew up as a guide and cook for treks in the Bob Marshall Wilderness. She has a family history that dates back to the Bannack gold rush days of 1863. From Bannack, Jean's great-grandfather followed the gold rush to a mountain camp called Diamond City above White Sulphur Springs. Later he moved to the valley town of White Sulphur Springs and became involved in the territory's commercial and political life.

Jean's grandmother broke new ground as well. Fanny Y. Cory was the first woman to have a syndicated cartoon. Her appearance in Harper's Magazine was not recognized as the contribution of a female. She found her work easier to sell if publishers thought she was male with the initials F.Y. Cory. In Montana, F.Y. Cory is best known as a children's illustrator in books like her *Fairy Alphabet*.

Montana Mountain Lodge has five bedrooms, each with a private bath. Nature decorates the rooms with sunlight, stars and the scent of pine. A grand bedroom on the main floor has a private sideyard with a southern exposure. Or you can choose a cozy room tucked under the eaves. Peaceful nights bring only the lullaby of the wind whispering in the Ponderosa pines.

A steaming cup of coffee and tantalizing Pioneer Sausage Gravy with Biscuits bring your morning senses into focus. The Chicken Provençe is a favorite from Jean's catering menu.

Country Gravy

½ pound spicy bulk sausage
¼ cup all purpose flour
2 cups milk
salt to taste
¼ teaspoon ground pepper

Cook sausage in medium saucepan until browned, stirring to crumble. Drain all fat except about 2 tablespoons.
Stir in flour. Cook, stirring constantly until thick and bubbly. Wisk in milk, salt and pepper. Cook, stirring constantly for about 5 minutes. Serve over biscuits. Top with fresh parsley. Garnish with fruit. Serves 5-6.

Chicken de Provençe

6 chicken thigh and leg pieces
white wine
1 large onion
3 carrots, chopped
3 ribs celery
3 cloves of garlic
2 tablespoons dried herbs de Provençe
 (choice of dried herbs include rosemary, thyme, basil and parsley)
½ teaspoon salt
1 teaspoon white pepper

heavy cream
2 tablespoons flour

Place chicken in a Dutch oven. Add onion, carrots, celery and garlic. Cover with white wine. Cover and place in 325°F oven until chicken is done, about 2 hours. Remove chicken from pan and set aside. Heat sauce to a boil and reduce by 1/3. Mix cream and flour, add to boiling sauce and cook until thickened. Place chicken on a bed of noodles or rice. Pour sauce over chicken and serve.

Hostess: Jean Cooney Roberts
Address and Contact Numbers:
1780 Highway 89 North, White Sulphur Springs, MT 59645
1-800-631-4713, 1-406-547-3773
e-mail: mtlodge@ttc-cmc.net

Castle Museum

The Castle Museum is a histori-cal landmark built by cattle baron, B. R. Sherman. Displays show the mining, ranching and Native American life of the sur-rounding valleys and mountain regions. Contributions were made by the families who live in the White Sulphur area.

Castle Museum

Address and Contact Numbers:
310 Second Avenue Northeast, White Sulphur Springs, MT 59645
1-406-547-2324

Skylodge

The vast meadows and streams of the Smith River Valley are a sportsman's paradise. Rafters, hunters and skiers find a luxurious vacation home at the **Skylodge Bed and Breakfast**.

The vibrant colors and themes of Debbie's quilts are an elegant bonus that travelers enjoy. Walls of the two common areas are decorated with these nationally featured artist pieces: "Local Color" characterizes Montana wildflowers and "Dormant Time" is a tree in winter.

Skylodge is perfect for teenagers. Grilled pizza and games in the large recreation room are enjoyable activities after a day of skiing at Showdown. The downstairs area accommodates up to sixteen people with queen beds and a private bath in each room. There are three bedrooms on the main floor. The kitchen is the heart of this home and Marc and Debbie enjoy preparing recipes from all over the world. The pear coffee cake is from *Cooking Light* and the rosemary potatoes are from the *Complete Vegetable Cookbook*. Homegrown herbs are used.

Quick and Easy Pear Coffee Cake

Combine and set aside:
2 cups flour
2 teaspoons baking powder
1 teaspoon cinnamon
½ teaspoon nutmeg
¼ teaspoon salt
¼ teaspoon cloves

Combine and blend:
1¼ cup brown sugar
⅓ cup vegetable oil
½ teaspoon almond extract
2 egg whites
1 whole egg

1¼ cups fresh diced pears
¼ cup dried currants

Combine dry and liquid ingredients. Add pears and currants. Mix well and spread in to a 9x13-inch greased and floured pan. Bake at 350°F for 35 minutes .

Oven-Roasted Rosemary Potatoes

6 large russet potatoes, cubed to ½ inch
¼ cup olive oil
2 tablespoons minced garlic
1 teaspoon dried rosemary
½ teaspoon salt
½ teaspoon pepper

Preheat oven to 425°F. Line large baking sheet with aluminum foil and brush with 1 teaspoon olive oil. Mix all ingredients except potatoes. Add potatoes and toss. Evenly distribute potatoes on baking sheet. Roast 30 minutes on one side, turn over and roast 30 minutes until crisp and brown on outside and soft inside.

Host and Hostess: Marc and Debbie Steinberg
Address and Contact Numbers:
4260 Highway 12 East, White Sulphur Springs, MT 59645
1-800-965-4305, 1-406-547-3999

"The Springs" Stage Coach Panorama

A view of Main Street, White Sulphur Springs, from the corner of Main and 3rd Streets.

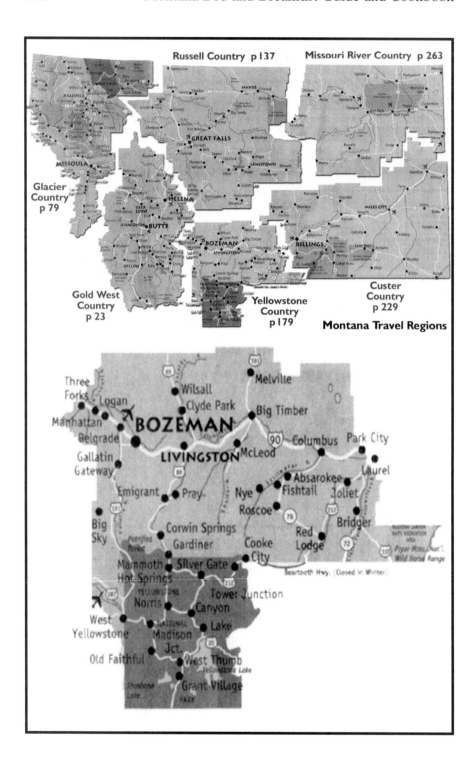

Russell Country p 137

Missouri River Country p 263

Glacier Country p 79

Gold West Country p 23

Yellowstone Country p 179

Custer Country p 229

Montana Travel Regions

Yellowstone Country

Yellowstone is another way of saying gold. And the gold in Montana's present-day Yellowstone Country is tourism. The Haynes Collection of historic photos, displayed at the Historical Society Museum in Helena, is about Yellowstone Park. These pictures show Yellowstone's legendary attractions. For over a century, world travelers have toured Yellowstone Park.

The crisp scenic beauty of the Gallatin Gateway and Paradise Valley parallels the geologic wonder of Yellowstone Park. Buffalo, dwarfed only by the magnificent Spanish Peaks, have reclaimed the meadows. Ranching is big business in the agricultural areas west of Bozeman. Cattle graze in the meadows and groves of trees punctuate the rolling hills where hay and grain are cash crops.

Not far away, shrieks of laughter and excitement echo through the canyons. Thrill-seekers ride the rush of white water in summer and master the moguls of Big Sky and Bridger ski resorts in winter. Several bed and breakfast homes provide rest and relaxation. Sauna, spa or whirlpool baths are available, soothing over-exerted bodies and aching muscles.

Millers of Montana

The **Miller's of Montana Bed and Breakfast** is located near Big Sky

Ski Resort in the Gallatin Valley. Joyce and Doug Miller celebrate a decade of serving travelers. It is delightful to wake up on a clear, crisp winter morning with the sun streaming through the east windows of the Peach Suite. Across the meadow, you see deer and rabbit tracks left after last night's snowfall. Straight ahead, a blue-green silhouette in the morning sun, are the Spanish Peaks.

Miller's is a modern Tudor-style home. It has separate controls in each bedroom so you can be cozy or cool. A breakfast nook, dining room and adjoining living room provide ample gathering space. Dried floral accents created by the hostess make the area look like a setting from the *Coun-*

try Living magazine. Colors appropriate to big sky country accent each room. There is the deep blue of the Big Sky, rich green of the Gallatin meadows, burgundy of a country Christmas and the wholesome golden color of homemade stuffed croissants or lemon bread.

Joyce's Divine Filled Croissants

4 large croissants, sliced length-wise
4 tablespoons butter
8 eggs
¼ cup milk
1 teaspoon basil
½ cup chopped mushrooms

½ cup grated Monterey Jack cheese
4 orange sliced for garnish
parsley sprigs

Melt butter in skillet. Scramble eggs with milk until creamy; add mushrooms and basil. Put eggs on sliced croissant, top with cheese, and
place under broiler until melted. Garnish with orange slices and parsley sprigs. Serve with fresh fruit platter.

Lemon Yogurt Bread

3 cups flour
1 teaspoon salt
½ teaspoon baking powder
1 teaspoon baking soda
1 cup finely chopped almonds
3 eggs
1 cup vegetable oil
1 ¾ cup sugar
1 pint lemon yogurt
1 tablespoon lemon extract

Preheat oven to 350°F. Sift together flour, salt, baking powder and
soda. Stir in nuts, set aside. Beat eggs in a large bowl, add oil and
sugar, cream thoroughly. Add liquid ingredients, yogurt and lemon
extract. Divide into two loaf pans. Bake covered with foil for 40
minutes and uncovered another 10 minutes or until golden brown.

**Host and Hostess: Doug and
Joyce Miller**
Address and Contact Numbers:
1002 Zacharia Lane, Bozeman,
MT 59715
1-406-763-4102
www.millersinn.com

Voss Inn

Standing graciously in Bozeman's Historic District is the **Voss Inn Bed and Breakfast.** Newlyweds, singles and families find accommodations only blocks from Main Street. German-born John C. Paulson

designed the Voss Inn. Historians know Paulson best for the architectural design of the regal Broadwater Promenade and Natatorium that stood on the outskirts of Helena.

Frankee and Bruce Muller, the innkeepers of the Voss, met

and worked in Botswana, Africa. Photography brought them together. Bruce was the guide for a photographic safari and Frankee was the photographer who needed guiding. Several careers, two children and a decade later find them happily operating one of Montana's finest and busiest bed and breakfast homes.

Distinctive Botswana baskets remind Frankee and Bruce of days in an earlier paradise. The baskets are for sale to Voss guests. Another distinction of the Voss is their afternoon tea. For breakfast, eggs are prepared in individual ramekins. You may have a breakfast tray and a carafe of coffee in your room or join other guests.

Fast Egg Casserole

For each ramekin:
1 egg
¼ cup milk
dash each of dry mustard, onion powder, salt, pepper
¼ cup of grated cheese, croutons, bacon bits combination
(for 5 ramekins use ½ teaspoon of each spice, for 10, use 1 teaspoon)

In bottom of ramekin place one layer of croutons. Sprinkle cheese over croutons. Mix egg, milk and spices. Pour over croutons and cheese. Bake at 350ºF for 22-25 minutes. Top with bacon bits. Muffin tins may be used but need to be well-buttered.

Host and Hostess: Bruce and Frankee Muller

Address and Contact Numbers:
319 South Willson, Bozeman, MT 59715
1-406-587-0982

Torch and Toes

The **Torch and Toes Bed and Breakfast** is as novel as its name. The
assemblage of the Statue of
Liberty, a gift to the United
States from France, did not
arrive posed to cry, "Give me
your tired, your poor." It came
in pieces; "the Torch" possi-
bly crated with "the Toes."

The careers and interests of
Ron and Judy Hess, owners of
the Torch and Toes, make
them good company for anyone curious about the world. Ron is a
professor of architecture and Judy is a weaver. They are both world
travelers. The Torch and Toes is reminiscent of a European homestay.

The architecture of the Torch and Toes combines Colonial Revival style
with classic interior accents like the detailed mantle piece in the dining
room.   Walls and nooks display American antiques and dolls collected from many lands. Art treasures from Russia add whimsy and
interest to the home. A full breakfast like baked blintz is delicious and
healthy.

Baked Blintz

Filling:
2 3-ounce bricks cream cheese
1 cup lowfat cottage cheese
1 egg, beaten
1 tablespoon sugar
1 teaspoon vanilla

Batter:
½ cup butter or margarine (room temp)
1/3 cup sugar

4 eggs
1 cup flour
2 teaspoons baking powder
1 cup plain yogurt
½ cup lowfat sour cream
½ cup orange juice
berry preserves

Preheat oven to 375°F. Butter and flour a
9x13-inch casserole dish. In a small bowl
beat cream cheese, add cottage cheese,
add sugar and vanilla, mix well and set
aside.

In a large bowl, cream butter and sugar. Add eggs one at a time, beating well. Add flour and baking powder. Mix in sour cream and yogurt
and add orange juice. Pour ½ of batter into prepared casserole dish,
layer in filling and top with remaining batter. Bake 40-45 minutes
until lightly browned. Slice into squares and serve with a dollop of
sour cream and yogurt; top with berry preserves.
Serves 8.

Host and Hostess: Ron and Judy Hess
Address and Contact Numbers:
309 South Third Avenue, Bozeman, MT 59715
1-406-586-7285, 1-800-446-2138
e-mail: tntbb@avicom.net

Lehrkind Mansion

The **Lehrkind Mansion Bed and Breakfast** has a strong stake in the past, present and future of Bozeman's Historic Brewery District. The preservationist nature of Christopher Nixon and Jon Gerster charge them with refurbishing an untouched mansion. Their appreciation for the past has inspired neighbors to cherish and restore buildings in a community that was losing its distinction to development and the elements.

Bozeman's brewery district is one of only five historic places like it in the United States. Julius Lehrkind emigrated from Switzerland to Iowa as a penniless stowaway. He came to Montana when it was still a territory. Gold brought people to Montana and good farmland kept them when the gold strikes ceased. The soil and moisture content of the Gallatin Valley were superior for the production of barley. The water from melting snow-capped peaks and the fat kernels of barley grown in the Gallatin Valley were the perfect combination for good beer. Time, circumstances and the barley harvest were ripe for Julius Lehrkind's adventure as a brewmeister.

As you take in the morning sun on the expansive grounds of the Lehrkind Mansion, you see the buildings that were part of the brewing operation. Railroad tracks ran adjacent to the granaries where the barley was milled and stored. The fermentation, brewing and bottling took place in a separate plaza of buildings near the granaries. The workers lived nearby in a little cluster of houses that retain the charm of bygone days. Lehrkind managed the business from his office in the mansion. He believed in fair labor practices and honored a forty-hour workweek for his employees. The beer was an advertisement unto itself and became popular throughout Montana.

The mansion has always been a single-family home. Chris and Jon purchase period furniture that closely matches the original family heirlooms. For example, the Lehrkinds enjoyed music; one of their treasures is a Regina 7 music box. The "platters" are tin discs that have a diameter of 27 inches; a favorite tune is the German Blue Danube Waltz. Other prized antiques include an 1885 chintz appliqué quilt and an 1899 Singer sewing machine.

Chris and Jon left Yellowstone Park and careers as rangers and naturalists to become host and historian of the Lehrkind Mansion. The guestrooms honor naturalists like Muir and Audubon.

Hosts: Christopher Nixon and Jon Gerster
Address and Contact Numbers:
719 North Wallace Avenue,
Bozeman, MT 59715
1-406-585-6932, 1-800-992-6932

Fox Hollow

Located in a hollow with a backdrop of the Bridger Mountains and acreage of herbs, flowers and little red fox is the **Fox Hollow Bed and Breakfast**. The home is elegant and luxurious, spacious and spotlessly clean. American art pieces from Helena's Cason Gallery distinguish the Fox Hollow host and hostess as art *aficionados*. Selected works are for sale.

All five rooms have private baths. Sequestered in the Carriage House, is a honeymoon hollow with an ambiance and schedule all its own. A small armoire with pink roses, delicately detailed by Nancy, the hostess of the Fox Hollow, is in the honeymoon suite. Lighting is subdued and a deep jacuzzi completes the suite.

In the main home the garden theme is tastefully repeated in a profusion of pansies and stripes, roses and wreaths. You might guess that the Garden

and Meadow rooms have windows overlooking acres of gardens and meadows with walking paths and benches for enjoying the Bozeman Valley. Another rustic bedroom, called the Peaks, has a bear motif and windows with a view of the Bridger Mountains. Nancy and Michael prepare a full gourmet breakfast and goodies that equal the elegance of the home. The Black and White Cookies are from the *Choclatier*.

Oven-Puffed Pancake with Fruit Topping

½ cup flour
2 tablespoons sugar
¼ teaspoon salt
½ cup milk
2 eggs
2 tablespoons butter

Sauce:
½ cup sugar
1 tablespoon cornstarch
½ cup orange juice
1 tablespoon orange liqueur, or orange juice
3 cups variety of sliced fruits such as banana,
blueberries, blackberries, peaches, kiwi

Lightly spoon flour into measuring cup and level off. In medium bowl combine first five ingredients. Beat with wire whisk or beaters until smooth. Place butter in 9-inch pie plate and melt in oven just until it sizzles, 2-4 minutes. Remove pan from oven; tilt to coat bottom with butter. Immediately pour batter into hot pan and bake at 400°F for 14-18 minutes until golden brown. Must be served immediately as soon as out of the oven.

While pancake is baking make sauce. Combine sugar and cornstarch in a small saucepan. Stir in orange juice and liqueur. Stir and cook over medium heat until mixture thickens, about 7 minutes.

Remove pancake from oven, split in half, arrange fruit, dust with powdered sugar and drizzle with orange sauce. Serves 2.

Black and White Cookies

2½ cups flour
½ teaspoon salt
1 cup unsalted butter
¾ cup sugar
1 large egg at room temperature
2 teaspoons fresh, grated orange zest
1 teaspoon vanilla
4 ounces Hershey's semi-sweet chocolate chips, melted
4 ounces white chocolate, melted

Combine sugar and butter. Add egg and vanilla. Combine with mixture of flour and salt. Add orange zest and mix thoroughly. Place dough into pastry bag fitted with plain #4 or #5 tip. Pipe 2½-inch strips onto baking sheets about 1 inch apart. Bakeat 350°F for 8-10 minutes. Cool cookies on sheet on wire rack for about 1 minute. Transfer to rack and cool completely. Using two pastry bags fitted with ⅛ inch tips fill with chocolate, one white, one Hershey's. Pipe random lines of semi-sweet chocolate over cookies. Repeat with white chocolate. Store cookies in airtight container at room temperature for up to 5 days. Makes 4½ dozen cookies.

Host and Hostess: Nancy and Michael Dawson

Address and Contact Numbers:
545 Mary Road, Bozeman, MT 59715
1-406-582-8440, 1-800-431-5010
www.bozeman-mt.com
e-mail: foxholow@bozeman-mt.com

Bear Comforts Quilt Shop

Owner: Sandy Taylor

Address and Contact Numbers:
126 East Main, Bozeman, MT 59715   1-406-586-6097
email: bearcomforts@avicom.net

Bridger Inn

Ray and Patti Carkeek are ranchers and equestrians from the Madison Valley near Bozeman. A passion for ranching is evident in the many avocations of this couple. They currently own and operate the **Bridger Inn Bed and Breakfast** home on the highway to the Bridger Ski Resort.

Horses and hounds have roaming rights on the fenced acreage at Bridger Inn. The boardwalks, trellis, rose and rock terraces and meadows with fruit trees give guests many ways to enjoy this private country inn. All six guestrooms have queen beds and private baths and four have a private entry. The separate themes for each guest area highlight treasured collectibles. They include art from Bali, Navajo weavings from the South-

west, Oriental accents from Japan, trophies from an African safari, Western art by their friend Gary Carter and a variety of depression-ware antiques.

Ample amounts of moisture make the Bozeman Valley an ideal place to grow sour cherries for pies and syrup. For breakfast, Patti creates cherry syrup to accompany pancakes or blintzes.

Cherry Pancake Syrup

The basic proportions are:
1 cup cherries
2 cups water
1 cup sugar

Pick, clean and remove pits from desired portion of cherries. Bring water to boil in a pasta maker, a pot that has a removable strainer inside. Place fruit in boiling water and continue to boil until cherries are pulpy and have lost their juice. Remove inner strainer from boiling liquid and add sugar. Bring juice to low simmer and cook until syrup is of desired consistency. Serve hot over pancakes or blintzes.

Host and Hostess: Ray and Patti Carkeek
Address and Contact Numbers:
3691 Bridger Canyon Road, Bozeman, MT 59715
1-406-586-6666, 1-888-300-0666

Silver Forest Inn

Standing like a sentinel in a thicket of evergreen is the **Silver Forest Inn Bed and Breakfast**. It is a quarter mile from the Bridger Bowl Ski area. Arthur McKinney's dream of building a road and artist retreat was started in 1932. An out-door amphitheater and playhouse accompanied the Inn but has since been dismantled. Arthur McKinney died before realizing his dream. However, guests and residents enjoy the natural beauty, fresh air and solitude that McKinney treasured.

This area is historically significant. Before building the Inn, only a cutoff from the Old Bozeman Trail existed. A road through Bridger Canyon replaced the wagon ruts and horse trails. Arthur McKinney

named his hideaway the Flaming Arrow after the Flaming Arrow Peace Treaty that established a temporary truce between the Nez Perce and the Sioux along the bloody Bozeman Trail.

The Silver Forest Inn is simply decorated. Items like a rustic harness with tooled leather and bells remind guests of the history of the Inn. Willow wood seats and leather chairs and couches surround the

hearth fire. A cup of coffee is perfect company while you gaze over the panorama of the Bridger Mountains and contemplate a delicious breakfast.

Cream Biscuits

2 cups all purpose flour
1 teaspoon salt
1 tablespoon baking powder
2 teaspoons sugar
1-1½ cups heavy cream
1/3 cup melted butter

Preheat oven to 425°F. Use an ungreased baking sheet large enough for a dozen biscuits. Combine the flour, salt, baking powder and sugar in a mixing bowl. Stir the dry ingredients with a fork to blend. Slowly add 1 cup of the cream into the dry mixture, stirring constantly. Gather the dough into a ball and knead. If the dough seems dry and pieces are falling away, slowly add enough of the extra ½ cup of cream to keep the dough together. Place the dough on lightly floured board and knead for one minute. Roll or pat the dough into a square that is about ½-inch thick. Cut into 12 squares and dip into the melted butter so that all sides are coated. Place the biscuits 2 inches apart on the baking sheet. Bake for 15 minutes or until the biscuits are lightly browned. Serve hot with eggs and fruit. These biscuits are easily used as leftovers with a piece of meat or cheese for lunch or snacks.

Address and Contact Numbers:
15235 Bridger Canyon Road, Bozeman, MT 59715
1-406-586-1882, 1-888-835-5970
www.silverforestinn.com.

Howlers

The **Howlers Bed and Breakfast**, located in the foothills of the Bridger Range, is an open-air sanctuary for abandoned wolf pups. A ten-foot

electric fence encloses three acres of natural habitat where the eight wolves can feed and wander.

The timber wolf, exemplified in art and poetry, is a Montana totem of legendary proportions. The extensive research and development needed to operate a private sanctuary provides a rare and interesting opportunity for guests at the Howlers.

Sometimes honored, some-

times feared, the wolf is always an engaging topic of conversation. The Howlers are no exception. Cuszack, the Alpha male, is the most photogenic. Chief is handsome and striking because of his black and silver-streaked coat. Cheyenne, the Alpha female, is endearingly coy and is nicknamed "Shy-Shy." These wolves know the quality of their bed and breakfast accommodations and show no desire to wander.

The Howlers has gracious details that make it a home you will want to visit repeatedly. For example, the bathrooms are spacious with heated floor tiles and large tub and shower areas. Jan sends skiers off with a full breakfast featuring French toast from the Pentwater Bed and Breakfast in Michigan. They return with aching muscles and low energy levels only to revive in the guest spa with its fully equipped weight room and sauna. There  is also a wide choice of videos to watch in the big screen room.

Skier's French Toast

2 tablespoons corn syrup (light, dark, or combination)
½ cup butter
1 cup brown sugar, packed
1 loaf white bread, thickly sliced
5 eggs
1½ cups milk
1 teaspoon vanilla
¼ teaspoon salt

In a small saucepan combine the syrup, butter and brown sugar; simmer until syrupy. Pour this mixture into a 9x13-inch baking pan. Set aside. Slice the loaf into thick slices, remove crusts, and place on the syrup in the baking pan. Set aside. In a large bowl, beat together eggs, milk, vanilla, and salt. Pour evenly over the bread. Cover and refrigerate over night. Bake at 350°F uncovered for 45 minutes. Cut into squares and serve with bratwurst and a combination of fruit compote.

Montana Cinnamon Bread Custard

16 slices of cinnamon-raisin bread
1 stick butter
4 whole eggs
2 egg yolks
¾ cup granulated sugar
3 cups milk
1 cup heavy cream
1 tablespoon vanilla extract
confectioner's sugar
1 cup Montana huckleberries
1 cup raspberries
1 cup strawberries, sliced
1 cup combination of raisins and sliced
   apples

Preheat oven to 350°F. Remove bread crusts. Brush both sides of each bread slice with butter and arrange in rows in a buttered 9x13-inch baking dish. In a large bowl, beat together the whole eggs and egg yolks. Whisk in the granulated sugar, milk, cream and vanilla. Strain the custard mixture over bread slices. Place the baking dish in a roasting pan and pour in enough warm water to reach ½ way up sides of baking dish. Bake in upper third of oven for 25 minutes, or until the top is lightly browned and custard is set. Transfer to a rack and cool for 15 minutes. Cut into squares, sprinkle lightly with confectioner's sugar and serve with berries in season.

Host and Hostess: Dan and Jan Astrom
Address and Contact Numbers:
3185 Jackson Creek Road, Bozeman, MT 59715
1-406-586-0304, 1-888-469-5377
Location:
Take I-90 to Jackson Creek, Exit 319, 12 miles east of Bozeman. Go north 3 miles.

Gibson-Cassidy House

A drive along picturesque country roads through the mountains will take you from the Bridger Ski area to the Shields Valley. Winding its way to the Yellowstone River Valley is the Shields River. Wheat and barley fields, waving like amber blankets in the summer sun, surround the

ranch sites and cottonwood groves along the river. On the edge of Clyde Park, a little community in the middle of the Shields Valley, is the **Gibson-Cassidy House Bed and Breakfast.**

The Gibson-Cassidy prairie home was in disrepair until Nancy Gilbert's restorational talents brought it back to life. Three beautiful stained glass windows of green, orange and leaded crystal are restored and the

oak wainscoting is refurbished. Friends and relatives have donated antiques to the house in the spirit of historic preservation. Gibson-Cassidy has a modern kitchen. Nancy also operates a trendy clothing outlet for adults and children from the Gibson-Cassidy House.

The Wild Rice Breakfast Quiche is Nancy's original recipe and one that other bed and breakfast owners enjoy serving to their guests.

Wild Rice Breakfast Quiche

1 unbaked pastry shell
½ cup fully cooked ham, bacon, or Canadian bacon
½ cup chopped onion
1 tablespoon butter
½ cup shredded Monterey Jack cheese
½ cup shredded cheddar cheese
1 cup cooked wild rice
3 eggs
1 cup half and half
salt, garlic and pepper to taste

Bake crust at 425°F for 5 minutes. Sauté ham or bacon with onion. Spoon into crust and add rice and cheese. Whisk eggs with cream and seasonings. Pour into crust and sprinkle with Parmesan cheese. Bake at 325°F for 30 minutes. Serves 4.

Hostess: Nancy Gilbert
Address and Contact Numbers:
Box 5, Clyde Park, MT 59018
1-406-686-4490

Greystone Inn

Dedication to detail is seen in the restoration of the **Greystone Inn Bed and Breakfast** in Livingston. The hand-quarried sandstone for which the Greystone is named is found along greycliffs of the Yellowstone River. Gary and Lin, your host and hostess, have accurate information  about preserving vintage homes and identifying antiques. Russell Chatham is a well-known Livingston artist. Lighting at the Greystone enhances the ethereal quality of his landscapes.

The Greystone has only one guestroom and it has a private bath. The furnishings include original wallpaper with its repeating wreath of roses and peonies, rich walnut and oak mantles, pocket doors, and amber Fostoria crystal. Lin enjoys making Abelskivers. They are prepared in a special skillet and look like large golden donut holes.

Abelskivers

3 eggs, separated
3 tablespoons sugar
½ teaspoon salt
2 cups buttermilk
2 cups flour
1 teaspoon baking soda
3 tablespoons melted butter

Beat egg yolks until light; add sugar, salt and buttermilk. Add flour sifted with soda and baking powder. Fold in stiffly beaten egg whites. Heat abelskiver pan, melting ½ teaspoon butter in each cup. Fill 2/3 full of batter and with a skewer; keep turning abelskivers until they are golden brown. Makes about 22 abelskivers.

Host and Hostess: Gary and Lin Lee
Address and Contact Numbers:
122 South Yellowstone, Livingston, MT 59047
1-406-222-8319, 1-406-222-8350

Blue-Winged Olive

Follow highway 89 south of
Livingston along the Yellowstone River and you will come
to Paradise Valley.   At its
southern end is the Gardiner
entrance to Yellowstone Park.
Many fine bed and breakfast
homes are found in Paradise
Valley.   Three miles south of
Livingston is the Blue-Winged Olive.

The **Blue-Winged Olive Bed
and Breakfast** is as unique as
its name and as warm as its
auburn-haired hostess. Joan is
a watercolor artist schooled in
Japan. She is also a fly-fisher
who enjoys guests who share
her interest in angling. If you
are a fisher, you know that the
blue-winged olive is a lure
named for a mayfly that attracts the choicest fish. Joan's guided fishing excursions can become a gourmet event if you request a lunch to
accompany the guiding.

All four rooms in this modern
ranch-style home have private
baths. The dining area has two
tiers. One tier accommodates
a group of guests while other
guests gather for a presentation on angling, travel or watercolor painting.

Blueberry Griddle Cakes

1¼ cups flour
3 teaspoons baking powder
1 tablespoon sugar
1 egg
1 cup milk
2 tablespoons melted bacon
drippings

Sift flour, baking powder, sugar and salt together. Combine egg, milk and bacon grease. Combine thoroughly with dry ingredients. Allow to stand for 30 minutes. Add milk if batter is too thick to pour easily. Bake on griddle; before turning, dot with blueberries and flip.

Hostess: Joan Watts
Address and Contact Numbers:
5157 Highway 89 South, Livingston, MT 59047
1-406-222-8646, 1-800-471-1141

River Inn and Sheepherder Wagon on the Yellowstone

Spring arrives and the Yellowstone River bustles with activity. Built in 1895 as a farm home, the
River Inn Bed and Breakfast is one of the original homesites on the Yellowstone River. The barn is used as a commercial nursery where trees and shrubs are sold to the community.

Touches of the Southwest contribute to the uniqueness of the bedrooms. However, their names commemorate people and places of the Yellowstone. For example, the Absaroka Room has breath-taking views of the mountain range of the same name. The Yellowrock Room overlooks the Yellowstone River from its private deck

Artifacts from all over the world add whimsy to the great room and the dining area. Among the treasures is a set of Marshall Ware with its earthy ochre, green and ebony accents. Refurbished pine floors add authentic charm to this friendly farmhouse on the banks of the timeless Yellowstone River.

Greek Egg Strata

1 6-ounce can diced green chiles
2 large slices of bread
10-12 fresh farm eggs
2 tablespoons sour cream
1 tablespoon favorite mustard
4 ounces of feta cheese
fresh tomato chunks
fresh oregano and/or basil
1 medium onion
½ teaspoon red pepper
mushrooms or other vegetables
½ teaspoon salt

The night before serving, sauté onion, pepper, mushrooms, and other vegetables. Combine with salt and herbs. Butter 5x10 baking dish and cover bottom with green chiles. Cover chiles with bread slices. Cover bread with sauté mixture. Mix eggs, sour cream and mustard. Pour over layers. Combine feta cheese and tomato chunks; spread over strata. Refrigerate overnight. Bake for breakfast at 350°F for 45 minutes.

Dotty Spangler's Sheepherder Wagon

If you really want to experience life on the timeless banks of the Yellowstone River, ask for **Dotty Spangler's Sheepherder Wagon**. Akin to the horse-drawn cov-
ered wagon of the pioneers, Dotty's Western Winnebago catered to the shepherdess with an intellectual bent. The rustic wagon contains a built-in secretary replete with yellowed stationery and books that were popular at the turn

the century. Reading and writing offered diversion to the solitary life of a shepherdess. Be warned that the wagon does not have a private bath. However it has abundant privacy for an artist or writer-in-residence who needs to concentrate, and it has a roaring river at its doorstep to drown out any other sounds of the world.

Shepherdess Pie

2 cups leftover mashed potatoes
½ pound hamburger
¼ pound ground pork
½ teaspoon pepper
½ teaspoon salt
¼ cup finely minced onion
½ teaspoon marjoram
½ teaspoon thyme
1 cup cooked garden peas

Fry hamburger and ground pork, drain grease. Add onion and sauté. Add spices, mix thoroughly with meat. Lightly grease a 1½-quart casserole. Line the bottom of dish with layer of 1/3 of mashed potatoes. Layer with ½ meat, and ½ of the peas. Repeat layer and close over with last 1/3 of mashed potatoes. Sprinkle with paprika. Bake at 400°F for 40 minutes.

Hostesses: DeeDee Van Zyl and Ursula Neese
Address and Contact Numbers:
4950 Highway 89 South, Livingston, MT 59047
1-406-222-2429
www.wtp.net/go/riverinn
e-mail: riverinn@wtp.net

Johnstad's

A Lutheran minister and his wife acquired land in Paradise and built a bed and breakfast home. Ron and Mary Ellen Johnstad are retired. They fondly reminisce about their first flock and pastorate in Shields Valley in a book called *Montana As I Remember It.*

The **Johnstad's Bed and Breakfast** commemorates people, family and a Norwegian heritage. Norwegian folk art called rosemalling decorates the kitchen and the Heritage Room. Miniature porcelain Lomonosov bears from Russia, American depression ware and an antique washstand accent the spacious dining area. The Yellowstone River is only two hundred yards away.

Paradise Strawberry Pie

¹/₃ cup shortening
1 cup flour
¼ teaspoon salt
3 tablespoons water
1 package strawberry junket
2 cups cold water
½ cup sugar
3-ouncepackage strawberrry
Jell-O

Pie Crust:

Cut $1/3$ cup shortening into salt and flour mixture. Blend until crumbly and shortening is evenly distributed through flour. Add enough water to cause flour mixture to clump. Form into ball and roll between two pieces of waxed paper to 9-inch pie shell. Place raw dough over pie tin that is up side down. Prick with fork to avoid bubbles when baking. Bake for 5-10 minutes at 400°F or until light brown. Cool and carefully place in 10-inch pie dish. An alternative method would be the use of a spring-form pan to bake the raw pie crust.

Filling:

Combine junket, water, and sugar. Bring strawberry mixture to a boil and add ½ of 3-ounce package strawberry Jell-O. Boil this mixture for 1 minute. Cool mixture until it starts to jell. Put ¼ of Jell-O mixture into the bottom of baked pie shell. Place whole, fresh strawberries over the entire bottom of pie shell until full. Spoon remaining Jell-O mixture over the berries. Note: Norwegians eat this pie for breakfast so it is acceptable to refrigerate the pie overnight and serve it with whipped cream in the morning.

Host and Hostess: Ron and Mary Ellen Johnstad

Address and Contact Numbers:
Box 981, 03 Paradise Lane, Emigrant, MT 59027
1-800-340-4993, 1-406-333-9003,
www.wtp.net/go/johnstad
e-mail: rjohnstad@aol.com

Paradise Gateway

The **Paradise Gateway Bed and Breakfast** is near the little town of Emigrant, Montana. Emigrant Gulch is named for a spirited band of pioneers who took the Bozeman Trail west in 1864. On a whim, three of the men in the party explored the gulches and ravines above the Yellowstone River. They discovered gold; a brief boom followed. More importantly, these emigrants settled in the valley and named the area for the yellow stone that was so important to their success.

The pioneering spirit remains alive with homesteaders who settled above Emigrant Gulch. Agnes is the Culinary Queen of the Valley, known for her delicious pies and caramel rolls. Agnes came to the valley as a young school marm when Emigrant had a one-room school. That was sixty-five years ago.

Carol and Pete Reed, the owners of Paradise Gateway, are enthusiastic promoters of Emigrant, Paradise Valley and Yellowstone Park. "Welcome" is part of caring for bed and breakfast guests as well as the many friends and neighbors who drop by to visit. Four rooms with private baths are available for families, parties of fishers, locals on a get-away from home and tourists who need a rest before an early start to explore Yellowstone Park.

The host and hostess are skilled at everything from building log houses to adorning walls with stencils and baking homemade bread and cook-

ies. Homespun quilts of natural fibers brighten each room.
Guests can also choose
accommodations that over-
look the Yellowstone River.
Two cabins are fully equipped
with a kitchen and other
amenities of home such as a
washer, dryer, phone and television. Their distance from a

variety of restaurants prompts requests in their home restaurant. These
recipes are among their favorites.

Asparagus Rollups

1 cup grated Colby or mild cheddar cheese
1 cup grated feta cheese
¼ cup grated sweet onion
1 teaspoon dill seed
½ cup real mayonnaise
1 loaf whole grain or white bread
12-18 spears of asparagus, cleaned with woody part of stem removed
½ cup melted butter

Combine first five ingredients and mix thoroughly. Slice loaf of bread
and remove crusts. Roll each slice flat with a rolling pin. Spread each
flattened slice with a portion of the cheese mixture. Place one asparagus spear in the middle of each slice of bread and cheese and roll into
a round. Place each round, seam side down, in a 9x13 baking pan.
Brush with melted butter. Bake at 350°F for 20 minutes or until lightly
browned.

Paradise Gateway Scones with Lemon Curd

2 cups flour
3 tablespoons sugar
¼ teaspoon salt
3½ teaspoons baking powder
²/₃ cup margarine
¹/₃ cup combination of raisins, blueberries, dried cranberries or chopped
  nuts
¾ cup milk

In a large bowl mix together flour, sugar, salt, and baking powder. Cut in margarine with pastry cutter or fingers until mixture resembles coarse oatmeal. Add berries or nuts and mix. Add milk. Mix lightly with fork until just blended. Add one or two additional tablespoons of milk if necessary to hold mixture together. Divide into two equal portions and turn onto a floured board. Pat into circles 1inch in thickness. Handle only enough to pat into shape. Score with a knife half way through to form four portions in each circle. Brush with 1 tablespoon milk. Bake for 18-20 minutes in 425°F oven until golden brown. For oatmeal scones, substitute ²/₃ cup of flour for ½ cup oatmeal and ¼ cup of coconut.

Lemon Curd
¾ cup sugar
grated rind from two lemons
¹/₃ cup lemon juice
½ cup margarine
3 eggs well beaten

Put all ingredients in top of double boiler over hot water. Stir until well blended and thick, only a few minutes over medium to low heat. Mixture thickens more as it cools. Spread over scones. Keeps for up to two weeks refrigerated.

Norwegian Rice Cream

1½ cups uncooked rice
½ gallon warm whole milk
1½ cups sugar
4 eggs
1 pint whipping cream
2 teaspoons almond extract

In a heavy saucepan combine rice, milk and sugar thoroughly. Simmer for about 30 minutes, or until rice is soft, stirring often. Beat the eggs and cream in a blender. Add the flavoring. Add the egg mixture slowly to the rice mixture and boil for 2 minutes. Serve warm topped with red raspberry sauce.

Host and Hostess: Pete and Carol Reed
Address and Contact Numbers:
Box 84, Emigrant, MT 59027
1-800-541-4113, 1-406-333-4063
www.wtp.net/go/paradise
e-mail: paradise@gomontana.com

Burnt Out Lodge

Burnt Out Lodge Bed and Breakfast is a typically Montana place to go. Even the names of the Burnt Out's owners, Blick and Ruth Drange sound like they came out of a Louis L'Amour adventure of the West. Ruth tells us, "Blick got his name when a sheepherder hung it on him; he was three and it stuck."

Burnt Out Lodge is an artistic lodge carved out of a mountainside because a fire burnt out the Drange forest. The process to save a burnout of logs needs to be done within eighteen months or the timbers begin to turn blue-black and decay. Again Ruth filled in the details, "A log wizard or shaving blade on the end of a chain saw is used to remove the burned bark. An electric rotary sander is used to finish and polish the logs before the building is started." The finished pine and Douglas fir logs have only a clear varnish because the rich golden color and burnished nature of the logs would be lost with a stain.

The Burnt Out Lodge is new. Five spacious and immaculately clean bedrooms are beginning to take on character as art and antiques find

their appropriate places. There is a room dedicated to the pioneering women of Montana and there will be one for the men. The lodge has a Western great room for community gatherings.

Mazette

2 pounds ground beef
2 cans tomato soup
1 package noodles
2 cans mushrooms
2 small onions
1 pound grated cheese
½ cup chopped green peppers

Cook noodles in salted water. Brown
meat and onions. Place in buttered baking dish as follows: Layer
noodles, meat, onions, mushroom, cheese, green pepper and tomato
soup. Bake at 350°F for 1 hour. Serves 6-8 people.

Host and Hostess: Blick and Ruth Drange
Address and Contact Numbers:
Box 3620, Big Timber, MT 59011
1-888-873-7943, 1-406-932-6601

Buckin' Horse Bunkhouse

Janis Maclean had a dream as a little girl growing up in Toronto, Canada. She wanted to be a cowgirl. Janis and her husband, Rod, have made that dream come true at the authentic and charming **Buckin' Horse Bunkhouse Bed and Breakfast**.

Rod is the owner of Logmaster Homes. Coupled with Janis' degree in fine arts, they are bound for success. That success has included an eye for Old Beacon Indian Blankets enhanced by logs selected for their burls. Janis makes log and padded leather furniture that parallels the talent of Thomas Molesworth. Cozy chairs and couches casually draw guests to curl up with a good book. Tiny birdhouses that mimic the look of the Bunkhouse attract feathered friends from the bunting family or from the variety of warblers that frequent the meadows around the Buckin' Horse.

The Bunkhouse is not far from the garden. A variety of berries and vegetables may appear on the breakfast menu. You might note that

you do not need to find a restaurant for other meals of the day. An outdoor barbecue and picnic tables are available for guests. Janis provides wood and charcoal. A creek flows at your feet and you may catch fish for lunch. The Buckin' Horse Bunkhouse is perfect for children and they are welcome.

Butter Tart Muffins

1½ cup raisins
¾ cup sugar
½ cup butter, cut into chunks
2 eggs, beaten
½ cup milk
1 teaspoon vanilla, rum, or but-
terscotch flavoring
1½ cups flour
2 teaspoons baking powder
1 teaspoon baking soda
¼ teaspoon salt
½ cup walnuts, chopped
¼ cup corn or maple syrup

Place raisins, sugar, butter, eggs, milk and flavoring in a large heavy-bottomed saucepan. Place over medium heat and cook, stirring frequently, until mixture is hot, slightly thickened and begins to bubble, about 5 minutes. Cool slightly in the refrigerator while continuing with remainder of recipe.

Preheat oven to 350°F. Grease 12 muffin cups or spray with cooking spray. Sift flour, baking powder, baking soda and salt in a large mixing bowl. Make a well in the center of dry ingredients and pour in warm raisin mixture, stirring only until combined. Stir in nuts until evenly mixed. Spoon batter into muffin cups. Bake in center of oven until golden brown. Test to see that center is baked when inserted toothpick comes out clean, about 12 minutes. Remove from oven and immediately pour 1 teaspoon syrup over top of each golden muffin. Cool in cup for 10 minutes, then remove to a rack. Serve warm. Store muffins in a sealed bag at room temperature for up to 2 days. For longer storage, refrigerate or freeze.

Host and Hostess: Rod and Janis Maclean

Address and Contact Numbers:
Box 521, Reedpoint, MT 59069
1-406-932-6537
www.buckinhorse.com

Riverhaven Bed and Breakfast

In a country cottage on the Stillwater is the **Riverhaven Bed and Breakfast**. Betty Oleson, the owner, spends her winter in the Southwest. In the summer months the Riverhaven beckons to river rafters and fishers who know the blue ribbon quality of the Stillwater.

Dianthus, French lilacs, poppies, tulips and pansies deck the boardwalks, gardens and paths around the Riverhaven. Indoors, the accents of tile, storyteller dolls, tapestries and watercolor by the hostess add conversation pieces to the tales of a world traveler.

Betty travels with the purpose of using new ideas at Riverhaven. For example, she participates in cooking schools and is a connoisseur of fine wines. She takes art classes and buys items like original weavings and decorative carvings that will enhance the guestrooms.

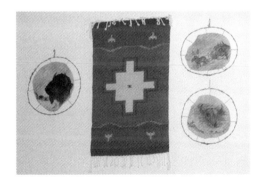

Chicken Eddy

4 cups cooked chicken, cubed
3½ cups (8 ounces) dry, uncooked spaghetti broken into
2-inch pieces
1½ cups chicken broth
3 cans cream of chicken mushroom soup
1½ cup diced onion
¾ cup diced green pepper
¾ cup diced red pepper or 6
ounces pimiento
½ pound cheddar cheese

Mix together all ingredients except cheese. Refrigerate overnight in 9x13-inch pan or casserole. Bake uncovered at 350ºF for 50 minutes. Sprinkle cheese on top and bake for 20 minutes more.

Hostess: Betty Oleson
Address and Contact Numbers:
Route 1, Box 2870 Absarokee, MT
59001
1-406-328-4138

Bear Bordeaux

The **Bear Bordeaux Bed and Breakfast** is the newest place to stay in Red Lodge. The most fetching detail of Sharon and Joe Torcaso's bor-

deaux is not a bear at all, but Sir Winston, a two-year-old golden retriever. Sir Winston will give you a wake-up call in the morning if you let him know the night before. He enjoys "sleeping in" if there is not work to do.

The unique name of the lodge matches its quality. The name was Joe's idea: Bear as the mascot of the Beartooth Range, and Bordeaux for a region in France known for its fine wines. A wine reception each evening allows guests the time to get acquainted with Sharon, Joe, Sir Winston and other guests at the Bordeaux.

The unique quality of the Bordeaux is a spin on Sharon's experience as a hotel management executive. She treasures the time to pamper guests. Her room decor expresses the personal best of the many ideas she encountered serving people across the United States. For instance, the spacious bathrooms include a variety of marble and other Italian tile. A 400-volume video library and over 3000 books offer entertainment after a day of shopping, touring or skiing.

Host and Hostess: Joe and Sharon Torcaso
Address and Contact Numbers:
302 South Broadway, Red Lodge, MT
1-406-446-4408, www.wtp.net
e-mail: bearbor@wtp.net

Willows Inn

The **Willows Inn Bed and Breakfast** is a bustling place where friends find warmth and family fun. Carolyn and Cody have strong Finnish and Italian ties to the community of Red Lodge. The Festival of Nations is an annual event in the first part of August that draws performers and guests from all over the world.

The Willows Inn is a Victorian mansion built by Otto Herranen, a businessman of Finnish heritage, who settled in Red Lodge. This painted lady's second owner was a milkmaid from Finland who set up a boarding house. The Willows was neglected until the Boggios realized its importance as a Red Lodge monument. It is restored from the main floor to the cozy private bed and bath on the third floor. The spacious common areas are adequate for entertaining groups of people.

Two cottages are attached to the Willows. They are colorful in their Finnish design. Some of the antiques were found on site when debris and falling timbers of old out-

buildings were removed. Rescued coal miners' helmets and cooking utensils add authenticity to the Willows.

"Finnish is spoken here." And guests at the Willows can always count on freshly baked goodies. The dear Finnish grandmother bakes daily. She and her daughter-in-law Carolyn work well together and their banter immediately puts guests at ease. Ham and Crepes is Carolyn's original recipe that appears in the *Christian Bed and Breakfast Cookbook*.

Ham and Crepes

4 eggs
1 cup milk
1 cup flour
½ teaspoon salt
1 tablespoon melted butter

Blend first four ingredients and add melted butter; let stand ½ hour. Fry on griddle using enough batter to make ten pancake-sized crepes. Note: To make orange crepes add ½ teaspoon orange extract and 1 tablespoon orange rind.

10 orange crepes
10 thin slices of Danish ham
1 3-ounce package cream cheese
3 tablespoons honey mustard
3 tablespoons orange rind
1 6-ounce jar orange marmalade
6 ounces fresh or canned whole berry
  cranberry sauce
orange slice garnish

Make 10 orange crepes and set aside. Mix cream cheese and honey mustard. Mix cranberry sauce and orange marmalade in a blender, store in a jar. Lay ham on crepe and spread with 2 tablespoons cream cheese mixture and roll. To serve, bake at 325°F for 15-20 minutes and top with jelly mixture. Garnish with twisted orange slices.

Host and Hostess: Cody and Carolyn Boggio
Address and Contact Numbers:
Box 886, 224 South Platt Avenue, Red Lodge, MT 59068
1-406-446-3913
www.bbhost.com:8008/willowsinn/

Inn on the Beartooth

As you leave Red Lodge on the way to Cook City, the **Inn on the Beartooth Bed and Breakfast** will catch your eye. It is an expansive log home with a view of the Beartooth Mountain Range. Jan and Bob Goehringer have been bed and breakfast owners for 15 years. Their first home was Candlewick Inn in Fort Wayne, Indiana.

Evidence of Jan's career as an interior designer is apparent. Lodge pole furnishings were designed for the Beartooth. Casements for the large windows attract the eye and you can look beyond to the majestic and formidable Beartooth Mountains of Yellowstone Park.

Mushroom Scramble will delight any breakfast gourmet. This microwave recipe produces very tender scrambled eggs. It has only 200 calories per serving.

Mushroom Scramble

½ cup chopped celery
¼ cup chopped onion
1cup fresh chopped mush-
rooms
8 eggs
¼ cup grated Parmesan cheese
½ teaspoon salt

In a 1½-quart dish mix the celery and onion. Microwave for
2 minutes on high. Top with mushrooms. Beat together the eggs,
cheese and salt. Pour over the vegetables and cover with plastic wrap.
Microwave 3 minutes on high.
Using a rubber spatula or
wooden spoon, break up the
cooked portions and push toward center. Cook 2 to 3 minutes more, breaking the mixture once or twice until thickened, but before the eggs reach

d e s i r e d
doneness.
Stir again,
cover, and let stand 2 to 3 minutes to finish cooking.
Serves 4.

Host and Hostess: Bob and Jan Goehringer
Address and Contact Numbers:
Box 1515, Red Lodge, MT 59068
1-888-222-7686, 1-406-446-3555

Circle of Friends

The motto of Dorothy Phillips, owner of the **Circle of Friends Bed and Breakfast** home is: "Arrive as a guest, leave as a friend." The broad expanses of river, road and pastureland brand the Circle of Friends as one of the best places to stable your horse and find lodging for yourself.

Riding lessons for interested equestrians are available. Over twenty acres in this irrigated farming valley are available for horseback riding and just plain horsing around. The cash crops grown in this part of Montana are alfalfa, pinto beans, barley and sugar beets.

Dorothy takes special orders for any diet restrictions; anyone can order lunches or dinners for a small charge. This is an invaluable service because the Circle of Friends is out in the country and not near

a variety of restaurants. A delicious full breakfast comes with the price of the room. Tolovana, a no-flour muffin, is a healthy specialty.

Tolovana

½ cup vegetable oil
2 tablespoons molasses
1 tablespoon vanilla
4 eggs or 8 ounces Egg Beaters
¾ cup brown sugar
2 cups bran
1 cup wheat germ
1 cup nonfat dry milk
1 teaspoon baking powder
1 cup nut and raisin combined
¼ cup honey

Mix ingredients. Fill tins ²/₃ full and bake at 350°F for 20 minutes.

Broccoli Salad

1 large bunch broccoli, cut into small pieces
1 bunch green onions, diced
½ cup raisins
1 small can crushed pineapple, drained
½ cup chopped walnuts
1 cup Miracle Whip
¼ cup sugar
1 tablespoon vinegar

Mix all ingredients. Chill and serve.

Hostess: Dorothy Sue Phillips
Address and Contact Numbers:
Route 1, Box 1250, Bridger, MT 59014
1-406-662-3264

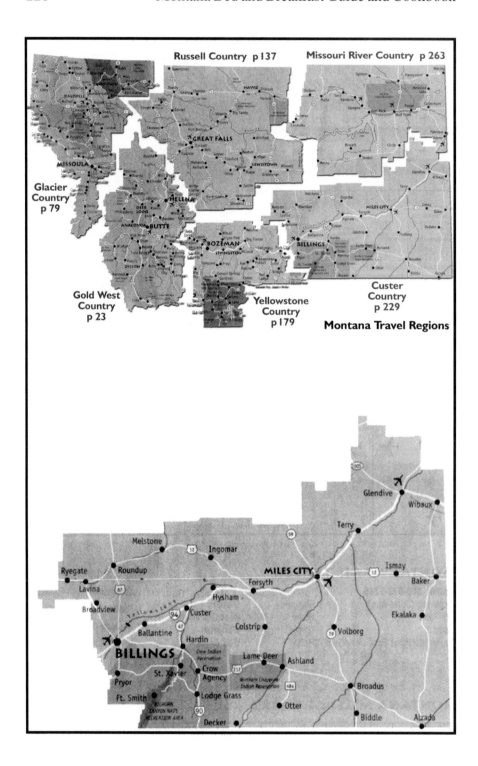

Russell Country p137

Missouri River Country p263

Glacier
Country
p 79

Gold West
Country
p 23

Yellowstone
Country
p179

Custer
Country
p 229

Montana Travel Regions

Custer Country

The southeastern corner of Montana is the heartland of the plain's economy. Custer Country remembers General Custer and his militia and their defeat at the hands of the Sioux at the Battle of the Little Big Horn. Prompted by industrial and military needs, riverboats and railroads contributed to the growth of places like Billings, Glendive and Miles City. Currently, farming, ranching and oil production and distillation are important to the economy of the area as are the production of alfalfa, wheat, barley and livestock.

Sanderson Inn

The **Sanderson Inn Bed and Breakfast** is located on the rolling hills outside of rural Billings. To the north are the Rimrocks, a residential vantagepoint, where you can view Billings and the surrounding valley. To the south, cottonwood trees along the Yellowstone are so thick they limit a view of the river bottoms.

Your hostess at Sanderson Inn is the gray-haired, soft-spoken, curious and strong-willed grandmother of all bed and breakfast hostesses, Margaret Sanderson. She is rightfully proud of her heritage as a sheep rancher. Margaret's ancestors crossed the plains from Missouri in the late 1800's and built the Sanderson House in 1905.

The Sanderson Inn is notable in its simplicity. Household details show a time of comfortable Missouri rockers, prized for their workmanship and comfort. Soft sheepskin rugs at each bedside remind you of the importance of sheep to this homestead.

The contemporary kitchen is separate but easily accessible to a large dining room that seats fourteen guests. The dining area overlooks the pastoral setting of sheep in the meadow and plum trees in full blossom. Margaret shares a poem by Janet Zedora, commemorating the centennial of Montana. These two recipes are favorites of guests at the Sanderson. The Chuck and Apples are from *Successful Farming*.

1889 - 100 years of 'Big Sky Country' - 1989

Hills and valleys
  so fertile and green,
Rivers and lakes
  so blue and serene.
The red and gold of the setting sun,
  paint a masterpiece that won't be undone.

From the peaks to the prairies
  wildlife abounds,
And the friendliest folks
  there are to be found.
Clear blue skies reign
  over this land,
That God has made with
  His loving hand.

By Janet Zedora, 1889-1989,
In Honor of Montana's Centennial

Homemade Bread

2 cups hot water
½ cup brown sugar
3 eggs
1 package granulated yeast
3 cups stone ground whole wheat flour
2-3 cups white flour
½ cube soft butter or margarine
2 teaspoons salt
½ cup powdered milk

Combine water, brown sugar, eggs and yeast. Set aside until yeast is active. Start adding wheat flour and mix well to build gluten. Add white flour until desired bread dough consistency is reached. Knead in butter, salt and milk powder. Turn and knead thoroughly. Let rise until double in size. Form into two loaves. Let rise and bake at 350°F for 25-35 minutes or until toasty brown.

Chuck and Apples

3 pounds boneless beef chuck, well trimmed
½ cup flour
salt and fresh ground pepper
¼ cup vegetable oil
2 cups apple juice
1 cup celery, sliced
1 envelope dry onion soup mix
3 cups apples, sliced
apple wedges
parsley or watercress

Cut beef into 2-inch cubes. Dredge in flour, salt and pepper to taste. Brown in oil in large frying pan. Stir in apple juice, celery and soup mix. Cover tightly and simmer about one hour or until tender, stirring occasion-ally. Add sliced apples and continue cooking, covered, until just tender, about 5 to 7 minutes. Transfer beef and apples to serving platter. Garnish with apple wedges and parsley. Spoon off fat from pan juices and serve juices with beef and apples. Serves 6-8.

Hostess: Margaret Sanderson
Address and Contact Numbers:
2038 South 56 Street West, Billings, MT 59106
1-800-314-3388, 1-406-656-3388

The Josephine

The **Josephine Bed and Breakfast** celebrates the colorful era of the riverboats. The steamers comprised Billings' first major source of revenue. With the advent of dams and railroads, the riverboat became obsolete but not forgotten. Becky and Doug Taylor, the owners of the Josephine, display pictures and antiques from the riverboat era throughout their vintage home.

The Josephine has continued to see exciting improvements every season. Its downtown location attracts business people. The Taylors have added equipment to help professionals do their job while they are traveling, including computer jacks for Internet access and fax machines to transmit reports and documents. Each of the five rooms has a private bath and the Castle Suite has a new luxurious whirlpool.

The downtown area, within walking distance of the Josephine, provides

entertainment and gourmet eating opportunities. The Moss Mansion and the Alberta Bair Theater are entertaining and Juliano's Restaurant is a gourmand's delight. Doug enjoys his role as morning chef at the Josephine and the strata and quiche recipes continue to be guest favorites.

Strata

8 slices toasted bread, cut into 1-inch cubes
8 ounces cheddar cheese, grated
8 eggs
4 cups milk

1 teaspoon dry mustard
¼ teaspoon onion powder
¼ teaspoon pepper
2 tablespoons bacon bits

Spray a 9x13-inch pan with nonstick spray. Sprinkle toast in bottom of pan and cover with cheese. Mix eggs, milk, mustard, onion powder, and pepper. Pour mixture over toast and cheese. Cover and refrigerate overnight. Bake at 325°F for 50 minutes, uncovered. Sprinkle with bacon bits and bake for 10 more minutes. Recipe may be made in 8 individual ramekins. Serves 8. Garnish and serve with fruit and muffins.

Easy Quiche Lorraine

1 eight-inch baked and cooled pie shell
1 cup Swiss cheese, grated
3 large eggs
1¼ cup heavy whipping cream
1 package ranch dressing mix
2 tablespoons bacon bits

Preheat oven to 400°F. Sprinkle cheese in pie crust. Whisk eggs until frothy. Add other ingredients and mix well. Pour over cheese. Bake 15 minutes at 400°F then reduce heat to 350°F. Bake 15-20 minutes more. May take 25-30 minutes until center is set. Cool for 10 minutes. Serves 8.

Host and Hostess: Doug and Becky Taylor
Address and Contact Numbers:
514 North 29th Street, Billings, MT 59101
1-800-552-5898, 1-406-248-5898
www.thejosephine.com
e-mail: josephine@int.net

Juliano's

Juliano's is not a bed and breakfast home; it is a five-star restaurant one block from the
Josephine Bed and Breakfast.
The elegant "Warm Soft Center
Flourless Chocolate Cake" was
contributed by culinary award-
winner, Chef and Owner Carl
Kurokawa.

Warm Soft Center Flourless Chocolate Cake

¾ pound butter
4 ounces dark bittersweet chocolate
10 egg whites
10 egg yolks
2 tablespoons vanilla
1½ cups sugar
¼ teaspoon salt
6 tablespoons cocoa powder

Melt butter and chocolate in double boiler. Whip egg whites to stiff meringue. Add yolks, vanilla, sugar, salt and cocoa powder to melted chocolate and butter. Whip 1/3 of meringue into chocolate. Fold in remaining 2/3
meringue with chocolate. Spoon into buttered ramekins and bake at 350°F
for 12-15 minutes. A bundt pan may be used; bake at 350°F for 60 minutes. Serve topped with whipped cream. For fancier presentation, garnish
with crystallized burnt sugar.

Address and Contact Numbers:
2912 7th Avenue, Billings, MT 59101
1-406-248-6400

Moss Mansion

The Moss Mansion is one of the most elegant museums of the Northwest and commemorates the illustrious Moss family. Ruth Towe, Executive Director, skillfully connects the mansion's extraordinary architectural details, period fixtures and antique furnishings with the history of Billings.

Address and Contact Numbers:
914 Division Street, Billings, MT 59101
1-406-256-5100

Pine Hills Place

Verne and Harry Barthuly are the owners of **Pine Hills Place Bed and Breakfast**. It is a tidy country guesthouse like a European homestay. Three large, homey units replete with snacking and cooking facilities are available. You can request homemade meals in addition to the full breakfast that comes with the cost of lodging. The kiln-dried pine beds are creations of the host. The pine wood blends with the colors of the patchwork coverlets created by Verne Barthuly. Geranium plants, star pine and poinsettias frame the windows.

The Billings area offers a wealth of interesting things to do. Within walking distance of Pine Hills Place is a ranch for renting riding horses and tack. The Indian Artifacts Museum is nearby. A public access to the Yellowstone

River allows floaters, kayak enthusiasts and fishers to use the river. Another alternative is to enjoy the surroundings at Pine Hills Place. A deck and hot tub look out on outcroppings of mossy shale. The side yard has a variety of trees and shrubs like the Ponderosa pine, lilac, column cedar, buckbrush and apple trees. The yard is home to wrens, bluebirds, Western warblers, magpies, chickadees and wild turkey. Cottontail, deer and squirrels are year-around visitors.

The Barthulys represent the heritage of Russia and Germany. They enjoy food from these countries and enjoy cooking in the European tradition. The exact ingredients of the German Cabbage Buns are provided courtesy of the author.

German Cabbage Buns

Dough:
¼ cup honey
2 tablespoons margarine
1 tablespoon salt
¼ cup mashed potatoes
¾ cup scalding milk
1 package yeast
½ cup warm water
1 egg
4-5 cups flour

Cabbage Filling:
¼ pound ground pork
¼ pound ground beef
1½ cups cabbage, shredded
¼ teaspoon dill seed

¼ cup onion, finely diced
1 large cooked potato, shredded
1 teaspoon salt
½ teaspoon pepper

To prepare dough, mix honey,
margarine, salt and potatoes.
Combine thoroughly with
scalded milk. Dissolve yeast in warm water. Combine with warm potato
mixture. Add beaten egg and mix thoroughly. Add flour gradually, beating
constantly until dough becomes sticky. Turn onto floured board, add flour
until dough is not sticky and can be formed into a loaf. Let rise, knead and
let rise again.

While the bread is rising, prepare filling. Fry pork and beef and drain ex-
cess fat. Sauté cabbage and onion with pork and beef; add potatoes, dill
seed, salt and pepper.

After kneading bread dough, divide into 15 pieces. Roll each piece large
enough to wrap around three tablespoons of filling. Place filling in center of
flattened dough. Pinch sides together. Place seam side down on cookie
sheet, about 6-8 to a sheet. Let rise and bake at 350°F for 20-25 minutes
or until golden brown.

Host and Hostess: Harry and Verne Barthuly
Address and Contact Numbers:
4424 Pine Hill Drive, Billings, MT 59101
1-800-238-9831, 1-406-252-2288

Toucan Gallery

The Toucan Gallery is a modern art gallery located in the renovated railroad district of Billings. The Toucan exhibits the work of Montana artists such as functional pottery by Christy Wert and fabric art by Laurie Gano.

Address and Contact Numbers:
2505 Montana Avenue, Billings, MT 59101
1-406-252-0122
www.toucangallery.com
e-mail: toucan@wtp.net

Kendrick House

The town of Hardin, Montana, is on the Big Horn River. Fishers, antelope hunters, photographers and artists note the wonders of the big sky in the colors and changing weather patterns. Hardin is in the heart of the Native American Crow Nation and borders the Crow Indian Reservation. Two bed and breakfast homes in Hardin welcome the traveler. They are central to visiting the Big Horn Museum, Chief Plenty Coups Museum, the Custer Battlefield and Pompey's Pillar.

The **Kendrick House Bed and Breakfast** continues to broaden its guest areas with the addition of a teahouse and antique shop. New lawns and gardens of delphinium, pansies, hollyhocks and ivy are in full summer bloom. The Kendrick House is a sturdy building of bricks and mortar over timber beams. The entry and porch along a southern exposure command the front of the house. Above it is a solarium for the guests. A handsome staircase

leads to seven guestrooms replete with transoms and individual sinks. Sconces glow brightly as dusk arrives and ceiling fixtures are of Victorian vintage.

The seven guestrooms incorporate a collection of historical memorabilia that inspire local residents to stop by and reminisce about the past. One woman remembers when she was a young chambermaid in the modern Kendrick Boarding House of 1915. Another woman remembers birthing twins when the home served as a hospital in the mid-1940's. Yet another, Jane Slattery, of

the Historic Hotel Becker Bed and Breakfast knows that she was born in one of the
Kendrick House birthing rooms.

The Lady Jasmine Tea House
and Antique Shop

*Marcie and Steve Smith, who
own and host the Kendrick
House, established the Lady
Jasmine Tea House. Marcie's
penchant for priceless antiques
shows in the elegance of an-
tique teacups and their replicas for serving custom-
ers. A basement antique shop is one of the premier
antique houses of southeastern Montana. Marcie
shares a popular French toast recipe.*

Peachy French Toast

3 eggs
3 tablespoons peach preserves
¾ cup half and half
6 slices French bread
1/3 cup peach preserves
½ cup softened butter or margarine
2 fresh peaches
2 tablespoons powdered sugar
2 tablespoons toasted almonds

In a small bowl, beat eggs and 1 tablespoon
peach preserves. Blend in half-and-half with
whisk. Place single layer of bread slices in
7x11-inch baking dish. Pour egg mixture

over bread, cover and refrigerate overnight or until most of liquid is absorbed. In a small bowl beat $1/3$ cup peach preserves and 4 tablespoons softened butter or margarine with mixer until fluffy. Set aside until ready to serve. At serving time, melt 2 tablespoons butter in a large skillet. Fry bread slices until brown, turning once. Serve toast with 1 tablespoon peach butter and fresh peach slices. Sprinkle with toasted almonds.

Host and Hostess: Steve and Marcie Smith
Address and Contact Numbers:
206 North Custer Avenue, Hardin, MT 59034
1-406-665-3035

Historic Hotel Becker

The **Historic Hotel Becker Bed and Breakfast** enhances the historical significance of Hardin's past. Mary and Jane Slattery, who were born and raised on a ranch in Hardin, open the Becker's doors every year in May. The interests and offerings of the Slattery Sisters and the Smiths at the Kendrick House complement one another and make downtown Hardin a tourist destination.

Train enthusiasts, ranch hands, baseball teams, quilters and berry-pickers enjoy the small-town flavor of the Becker. As Mary explains, "We're not fancy. We want to retain the working-man's interests in this bed and breakfast." Mary took the initiative to renovate the Hotel Becker because of the personal memories it holds for her. Mary and her dad would check how ranch hands fared as they wintered over at the Becker.

Remodeling the Becker to meet safety codes necessitated taking out an attractive old saloon that added character and held memories for Hardin folks. Mary has the original bar and can reinstall it if time and space permit. When you stop to visit the Becker, ask about the Undercover Gals and their wares in the back room!

The Becker has three rooms or suites, one with a private bath, and two rooms with adjoining bathrooms through a hallway. Homemade quilts are pert and pretty with patterns like the "Sawtooth Star," "Pine Trees," and "Apple Basket." Beside a variety of breads and jams at breakfast, Jane and Mary make and sell indigenous buffalo berry, chokecherry, gooseberry, wild plum, rhubarb, crab apple and wild currant jams and jellies that sell to a national market. Further information about domestic and wild prairie fruits are found in the *Rocky Mountain Berry Book*.

Almond-Cherry Streusel Coffee Cake

4 cups flour
½ teaspoon baking soda
½ teaspoon salt
4 teaspoons baking powder
1 cup margarine
1 1/3 cups sugar
2 eggs
16 ounces sour cream
2 teaspoons vanilla
½ teaspoon almond extract
1 cup milk
2 20-ounce cans cherry pie filling

Sift together and set aside flour, baking soda, salt and baking powder. Cream together margarine and sugar. Add eggs, sour cream, vanilla, almond flavoring and milk. Combine with dry ingredients. Grease springform pan.

Streusel Mix:
1 cup flour
6 tablespoons sugar
6 tablespoons butter
½ cup almonds, sliced and toasted

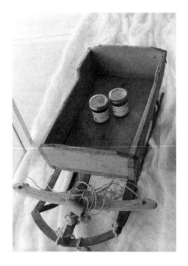

Combine flour and sugar. Cut in butter and mix in toasted almonds.

Spread 2/3 of batter into large spring-form pan. Spread pie filling on top. Dollop remaining batter. Sprinkle with sugar and nut mixture. Bake at 350°F for 1 hour. Cool for 10 minutes and serve.

Irish Soda Bread

4½ cups flour
3 tablespoons sugar
1 tablespoon baking powder
1 teaspoon salt
1 teaspoon baking soda
6 tablespoons butter or margarine
2 eggs
1½ cups buttermilk

In large bowl mix flour, sugar, baking powder, salt and soda with a fork. With a pastry blender cut in butter/margarine until mixture resembles coarse crumbs. In a cup, slightly beat eggs and reserve 1 tablespoon. Add butter-milk and remaining egg to flour mixture just to moisten. Dough will be sticky. Turn dough onto well-floured surface. With floured hands, knead about 10 strokes to mix thoroughly. Shape dough into a ball. Place in casserole. Use a sharp knife to cut a 4-inch cross into the dough about a ¼ inch deep. Bake at 350°F for 1 hour. Serve with Irish Stew. Tear off chunks or cut with an electric knife because soda bread will be crumbly.

Hostesses: Mary and Jane Slattery
Address and Contact Numbers:
200 North Center, Hardin, MT 59034
1-406-665-2707, 1-406-665-3074

Lakeview Bed and Breakfast

Did you know Colstrip, Montana, has a lake? And did you know Colstrip has **Lakeview Bed and Breakfast** with a tearoom and a gracious hostess? The news is out! The inviting aroma of a breakfast tearoom to wake you and the soft call of nightbirds when you sleep is not a secret anymore.

The ambiance of the home and tearoom transport guests to another land far beyond Colstrip. With artistic license, hostess Debbie Vetch uses places common to Colstrip to name her rooms. Castle Room takes its cue from Castle Rock. Knights of the Round Table and Ladies in Waiting portray the theme of the Castle Room. The grounds below the window include a groomed walker's path inviting a hike around the lake. After exploring, an invigorating soap and steam bath energizes any traveler.

The Woodland Room captures the essence of Colstrip's Canada geese and other waterfowl around the lakefront. The Garden Room wins the heart of a child with gnomes and fairy tales. They tell a story, underscoring the beauty of Colstrip's wildflowers and tended gardens. Selected verses from a poem by Marilyn Boese express her thanks to the Lakeview.

The Lakeview by Marilyn Boese, 1998

We're nestled on a lakefront
In a quaint coal mining town,
Where our bed and breakfast greets you
With uniqueness all around.

Aside from food and lodging
Our whole aim is to please,
With wholesome eats and chitchat
Coupled with our lake front breeze.

Within your choice of quarters
We cater every whim,
Your liking is our pleasure
And we'll fill it to the brim.

You can choose to socialize
And enjoy a cup of tea,
Or retire to your private space
And "pass" on company.

You come from all around the globe,
We'll miss you when you're gone.
Remember us to all your friends,
And pass the good time on.

We're glad you chose to stay with us,
We feel a special kin.
So if you're ever out our way
Please stay with us again.

Host and Hostess: Jim and Debby Vetsch
Address and Contact Numbers:
Box 483, 7437 Castle Rock Lake Drive, Colstrip, MT 59323
1-888-525-3262, 1-406-748-3653

Oakwood Lodge

The **Oakwood Lodge Bed and Breakfast** on Pumpkin Creek is near the small community of Broadus, Montana. It is known by locals as the "Doonan Gulch" settlement. Oakwood is a contemporary hunting lodge with a host and hostess who competently serve hunters, fishers and birders. An abundance of hospitality and game keep guests returning year after year. Four guestrooms with private baths are available.

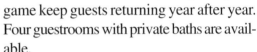

Russ Greenwood arranges the hunting camps and expeditions and Carol is the chef for retreats, meetings, workshops and parties that meet in the great room of the lodge. Oak timbers give the home its name and lend rich character to the rooms, especially with the light of the evening fire. Russ displays his trophies of black bear, ptarmigan, deer, elk, antelope and wild turkey bagged around Pumpkin Creek.

Birders hunting with a camera or adding new sightings to their birder's journal enjoy the Oakwood. The environs are alive with sedge hens, American goldfinch, pheasants, grouse, wild turkeys, meadowlarks and mountain bluebirds. The Greenwoods support local artists with a gift shop where guests can pur-

chase Fortner artist cards, wooden bowls and carvings, paintings and fishing tackle. Carol prepares meals for guests with reservations. Her homemade bread and the vegetables and omelet featured here are nourishing examples of fare at the Oakwood.

Mixed Vegetables

¼ cup oil
1 16-ounce can stewed tomatoes
1 cup beef bouillon
3-4 cups cubed, unpeeled zucchini
1 cup fresh or frozen peas
1 cup fresh or frozen corn
1 cup pared, sliced carrots
1 cup diced onion
1½ teaspoons salt
$1/_8$ teaspoon pepper

Place all ingredients in heavy cooking kettle. Cover and simmer 25-30 minutes. Let stand for several minutes before serving in small bowls. Pressure cooker may be used as an alternative method of preparation.

Host and Hostess: Russ and Carol Greenwood
Address and Contact Numbers:
Box 501, South Pumpkin Creek Road, Broadus, MT 59317
1-406-427-5474

Helm River Bend

The **Helm River Bend Bed and Breakfast**, owned by Pat and Gary Helm, is located on a wide bend of the Tongue River. The river is the source of life for a working ranch. Without it there would be no irrigation for alfalfa, malt barley, pinto beans or corn. The Helms raise alfalfa and corn for over one hundred head of registered Hereford.

The Helm River Bend has three rooms; one has a private bath and entry. The other rooms share a bath. The acreage along the river bottom supports an abundance of birds and big game. The Helm River Bend caters to people who have an interest in hunting. Bird and big game hunting packages are available. It is common to have the banter of

hunters around the dinner table as they share a successful day of scouting the fields and meadows by the river. Pat Helm cooks for hearty appetites.

Texas Style Potatoes

3 12-ounce packages frozen shredded hashbrowns
½ cup melted butter
1 teaspoon salt
¼ teaspoon pepper
½ cup chopped onion
2 cans cream of chicken soup
1 12-ounce carton sour cream

Topping:
¼ cup melted butter
2 cups crushed corn flakes

Thaw hashbrowns and mix with remaining six ingredients. Spread in 9x13-inch baking dish. Top with melted butter and crushed corn flake topping. Bake at 350°F for 45 minutes.

Quick Jell-O Salad

1 8-ounce carton Cool Whip
1 8-ounce can pineapple tidbits, drained
1 32-ounce cottage cheese
1 6-ounce peach Jell-O

Mix Cool Whip, pineapple and cottage cheese in bowl. Sprinkle dry Jell-O over mixture. Stir until Jell-O is dissolved. Put in serving bowl to set. This is simple and takes only minutes to prepare. Use other flavors of Jell-O for variety.

Host and Hostess: Gary and Pat Helm

Address and Contact Numbers:
Box 4161, Miles City, MT 59301
1-406-421-5420

Location:
On Highway 59 go 13 miles south of Miles City. Turn right on Tongue River Road. Go 5 miles to Helm Hereford Ranch sign. Turn right and go ½ mile to big yellow house on Tongue River Bend.

Charley Montana

An unconventional mansion called the **Charley Montana Bed and Breakfast** is a monument to ranching in Dawson County. This grand turn-of-the-century home memorializes the industrious Charles and Annie Krug family, who made their fortune in sheep ranching.

Charley Krug and his mansion embody the meaning of Montana at the turn of the century. When you stay at the Charley Montana you are on the Yellowstone River and can see the importance of the waterway to the existence of Glendive. Only a half-century after Lewis and Clark explored the Missouri at its confluence with the Yellowstone, steamboats were the most common way of reaching eastern Montana territory. Moreover, early territorial maps show Glendive as one of the main landings of the steamboats. With the advent of the rail, Glendive did not lose out. Steam-powered locomotives could take on enough water to go about one hundred miles; commercial sites grew where the engines stopped. Note that Glendive is about one hundred miles equidistant from Williston, North Dakota and Miles City, Montana.

Charles Krug began dreaming big. He worked on the Northern Pacific Railway and saw the changes taking place in Glendive. It was growing from a little town of shacks to a ranching center where merchants were involved in the burgeoning cattle industry. Krug began buying cattle and pastured them on the grasslands

that once supported herds of buffalo. Annals of Montana history note Charles Krug as a sheep rancher. Ultimately, it was in sheep that Krug made his fortune. The severe winter of 1886-87 obliterated Krug's cattle herd. With the money he banked, Charley bought sheep and resurrected his fortune.

A picture from the Montana Historical Society archives shows the main street of Glendive at the turn of the century. The boardwalks of the main street protect pedestrians from the mud and ruts of horse and buggy traffic. One block from main street, in the residential section, one property stands out. Charles Krug sought an architect and a plan for a solid mansion constructed of timber, brick and stone with space to raise a family of seven children. The el-

egant classical style was a break from the Victorian architecture common to mansions in the early 1900's. And it was important that the infrastructure withstand the ice heaves of freezing winters.

Katherine and Jim Lee are the host and hostess of the Charley Montana. Their preservationist philosophy allows only changes that are restorational

and can be undone. For that reason the old oak floors shine with an antique patina. The twenty-five rooms from the basement to the second-and third-floor guestrooms light up with prairie sunshine as they did when Charley Krug surveyed his mansion. Large pocket doors have never been marred and allow privacy or access to the parlours depending on the events hosted at the Charley. Coupled with eighteen-inch brick walls, transoms over many of the windows allow ample air circulation in summer. Two fireplaces enhanced with oak mantles and porcelain hearth tile are bright and warm in winter. There are hot water radiators throughout the mansion. The heating system was fueled by coal; the Lees use natural gas. Leaded glass dining room windows glisten with morning light at breakfast time and an expansive kitchen goes into high gear when the guest count for parties is over one hundred. Ranch Bread and Annie Krug's Goulash are from a yellowed parchment collection of Krug family recipes. It is an honor to include them here.

Ranch Bread

Mix and boil:
1 cup water
$1/3$ cup sugar
1 cup cooked ground beef
1 cup raisins
Allow above mixture to cool.

Soak:
2 packages granulated yeast
1 teaspoon sugar
½ cup warm water

Add:
½ cup potato water
3 tablespoons melted shortening
1 tablespoon molasses
1 cup all-bran cereal
2 cups graham flour
2 cups sifted flour

Add ground beef mixture. Let rise ten minutes.
Add:
3 teaspoons salt
½ cup walnuts
$2/3$ cup sifted flour

Knead 10 minutes. Let rise 10 minutes. Knead 5 minutes. Let rise until double. Punch down, and let rise to double. Makes one large loaf or two smaller loaves. Bake at 350°F for 40 minutes.

Mrs. Annie Krug's Goulash

2½ pounds ground beef
2 large bunches celery finely chopped
30-ounce can tomatoes
1 can tomato soup
1 red pepper
1 green pepper
2 pimientos
3 tablespoon crushed, uncooked
  spahetti
5 small onion, chopped
3 teaspoons salt
1 teaspoon chili powder
¼ pound butter
2 15-ounce cans kidney beans
mushrooms

Add easonings to meat. Toss meat 15 minutes in frying pan, add onions last 5 minutes, add pepper to suit. Use Crisco or bacon grease in frying pan. Add remaining ingredients to casserole, add ¼ pound butter and cook slowly for 2½ hours. Last 20-30 minutes of cooking time, add 2 cans red kidney beans. Do not cook the spaghetti before putting into casserole. If desired, add mushrooms last 5-10 minutes. Serves 20 people.

Host and Hostess: Jim and Katherine Lee
Address and Contact Numbers:
103 North Douglas Avenue, Glendive, MT 59330
1-888-395-3207, 1-406-365-3207

Hostetler House

The **Hostetler House Bed and Breakfast** is the home of Craig and Dea who grew up near Glendive. They have lived through much of its growth as a wheat and livestock ranch town. A visit to Europe and the charm of staying in bed and breakfast

homes in England inspired Dea to create a bed and breakfast home. The Hostetler House is the refurbished 1912 Bean home. The interior of this "Frank Lloyd Wright Prairie School" home is reminiscent of a four square bungalow, and twice its size. It has rich golden oak from the kitchen casements to the spiral staircase that opens to two quaint and handily decorated guestrooms.

Hostetler House, furnished with the heirlooms of a ranching ancestry, includes such detail as carved Amish dolls, Montana scenery in needlepoint and homemade quilts. A hot tub and gazebo are an extraordinary treat after a long day of travel. The potato casserole is served with a full breakfast. Breakfast at the Hostetler House always includes Dea's unique smoothie of juices and fruits in season. Along with a steaming cup of coffee or English tea it is an excellent way to start the morning.

Fruit Smoothie

½ cup frozen peach slices
½ cup fresh frozen strawberries
¼ cup fresh frozen blueberries
½ cup cantaloupe chunks
1 sliced banana
3 cups apple juice

Blend well, serve in a frosted glass, and garnish with a red strawberry with stem intact.

Potato Casserole

2-pound package shredded hash brown potatoes, thawed
¼ cup melted margarine
½ teaspoon salt
½ teaspoon pepper
1 can of cream of celery soup
2 tablespoons dried onion flakes
12 ounces sour cream
2 cups shredded cheddar cheese
1½ cups crushed unsweetened Cornflakes
¼ cup melted margarine

Mix all ingredients except cereal flakes and last ¼ cup margarine. Lightly grease a 9x13-inch pan. Add mixed ingredients. Cover with crushed cereal flakes and drizzle with ¼ cup margarine. Cover with foil and bake for ½ hour at 350°F. Remove foil and bake for ½ hour more.

Host and Hostess: Craig and Dea Hostetler
Address and Contact Numbers:
113 North Douglas Street, Glendive, MT 59330
1-800-965-8456, 1-406-377-4505
e-mail: hostetler@mcn.net

Pierre Wibaux Museum

Before you leave Wibaux on I-94, make an unforgettable stop at the Wibaux Museum. Pierre Wibaux, a Frenchman, is the town benefactor. The museum richly details the life of homesteaders who settled around Wibaux.

Address and Contact Numbers:
Box 74, East Orgain Street, Wibaux, MT 59353
1-406-769-9969, 1-406-795-2381

Nunberg's "N-Heart" Ranch

Fred and Shirley Nunberg of **Nunberg's N-Heart Ranch Bed and Breakfast** have the distinction of opening the first bed and breakfast home in Custer Country. N-Heart is seven miles south of Wibaux. It is a working ranch specializing in llamas. Fred, a remarkable artist in oil painting, started with monochromatic oils. Later he became fascinated with vivid colors. More recent paintings are so tastefully intense he is the "people's choice" artist in Custer Country.

There is a true story behind Fred's and Shirley's sausage and the N-Heart. Fred was an almost "dyed-in-the-wool" Polish bachelor when he asked his mother for the family Polish sausage recipe. His mother replied, "A wife is what you need, that's how you learn to make Polish sausage." Fred took his mother's advice to heart; soon friends "fixed his date with Shirley, they were married and Fred named his ranch the N-Heart to express how much he cared about his new wife." By the way, here is the sausage recipe . . . and Shirley's caramel rolls.

Fred's Polish Sausage

10 pounds ground beef
10 pounds ground pork
¾ cup Morton Tender Quick
2 tablespoons black pepper
2 tablespoons garlic powder
1 tablespoon sugar
1½ quarts warm water
1 pound size pork casings

Mix all ingredients except pork casings. Mix well and allow to marinate overnight. Keep refrigerated. Stuff into casings. Smoke in a smoke house or commercial home smoker of choice.

Shirley's Carmel Rolls

Dough:
8 cups of flour
3 cups of water
1-2 tablespoons of yeast
¾ cup sugar
1 tablespoon salt
2 eggs
¼ cup shortening
1/3 cup dry mashed potatoes
2 tablespoons gluten

Cinnamon Topping:
1 cup sugar
1 teaspoon cinnamon

Thoroughly combine cinnamon and sugar, set aside.

Caramel Topping:
½ cup margarine

½ cup sugar
½ cup vanilla ice cream
½ cup brown sugar

In a saucepan combine caramel ingredients over low heat until ice cream and margarine melt and ingredients are completely dissolved. Set aside.

For dough, mix 3 cups hot water and shortening; cool until mixture is warm, then add eggs. Mix sugar, salt, potatoes, yeast, eggs and gluten. Add to liquids and mix thoroughly until all ingredients are dissolved. Add flour gradually, beating constantly until dough becomes sticky. Turn onto floured board, add flour until dough is not sticky and can be formed. Separate dough into portions the size of a small dinner roll. Place side-by-side in 2 8x8-inch pans or 2 12-count muffin tins. Roll in sugar and cinnamon topping. Pour caramel topping over rolls. Let rise. Bake each batch at 350ºF for 20-30 minutes.

Host and Hostess: Fred and Shirley Nunberg
Address and Contact Numbers:
Box 7315, Wibaux, MT 59353
1-406-795-2345
e-mail: NunbergsBB@aol.com

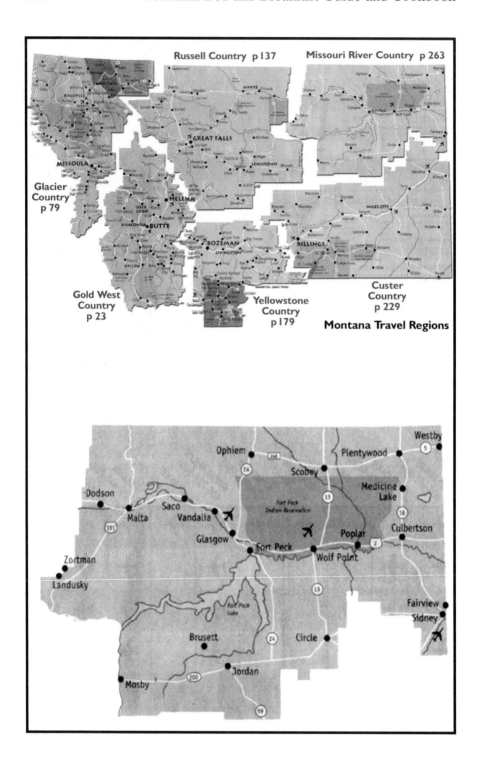

Glacier Country p 79

Russell Country p 137

Missouri River Country p 263

Gold West Country p 23

Yellowstone Country p 179

Custer Country p 229

Montana Travel Regions

Missouri River Country

The journals of Meriweather Lewis and CaptainWilliam Clark describe reaching the confluence of the Yellowstone River with the Missouri River in May of 1805. Their journey into the land that would become Montana Territory was marked by a cold spring. With the cold came wind, and the troop was able to put up sails and travel faster than before. Due to dams and irrigation, the present-day Missouri River of these plains is not as wide or navigable as it was in the days of the Lewis and Clark Expedition.

Antelope, elk, deer and even big horn sheep survive in the wilds around Fort Peck in present-day Missouri River Country. Lewis' journal describes the "horrid stench of mangled carcass." He is describing the mass of buffalo that met their death at a *pishkun* or buffalo jump near Judith gap. The Native American way of securing buffalo for meat and hides was to drive the stampeding animals over a cliff. In the spring vast numbers of hides were cured and sewn into clothing and teepees. The meat was boiled or dried. There are no herds of buffalo, in fact no buffalo at all, roaming the prairies of Missouri River Country today.

Meadowlark

The **Meadowlark Bed and Breakfast** is a butter-yellow frame and brick home located three miles from the Missouri River. Meadowlarks abound in the wheat and alfalfa fields of this three thousand acre ranch located near Wolf Point. A variety of activities enlarge your view of wheat ranching as you tour the tidy rural surroundings of the Meadowlark. You might pick up tips about homemade quilts from your hostess, Alice Whitmer. Or about Aga cooking as she turns out barrels of broasted chicken, barbecued ribs and apple pie when the bed and breakfast season coincides with the wheat harvesting of late summer.

Alice's ancestors lived in Cook County, Illinois until farming regulations prompted a move to homestead land on Chelsea Creek near the Missouri River. Times were good for the dry land farmer. Boone Whitmer's family also claimed a section of land as a wheat ranch.

This country ranch home is rich with local art and gracious rooms. C. R. Cheek is a Poplar artist who has painted a picture of the old homestead. The rooms include the Rose Suite which has a private bath and shower and a laundry, plus a kitchen and dining nook and its own patio. The Badlands Suite is fully equipped and can be enlarged for extra sleeping accommodations.

The Lewis and Clark Trail with the Nationally Historic truss bridge dedicated to the memory of the expedition is one of the celebrated land-

marks of Missouri River
Country. The Missouri River
breaks and the flora and fauna
so aptly recorded by Lewis and
Clark will be part of an interpretive effort as the bicentennial of the journey is com-
memorated.

The rib recipe from Alice is a work of culinary art. It takes time and
testing to get the balance of ingredients that please your palate. Not a
step is omitted so you can enjoy pork at its best.

Barbecue Ribs

Rub:
¼ cup light brown sugar
¼ cup white sugar
¼ cup seasoned salt
2 tablespoons garlic salt
1½ teaspoons celery salt
¼ cup sweet paprika
1 tablespoon chili powder
2 tablespoons fresh ground black pepper
1½ teaspoons sage
½ teaspoon cayenne pepper
¼ teaspoon ground cloves

Spread the brown sugar on a baking sheet and let dry out for an hour or
two to keep it from clumping. Then sift the sugar and remainder of rub
ingredients together in a bowl. Stir to combine. May use pulsar of
food processor to combine.

Sauce:
1/3 cup dark brown sugar
¼ cup white or apple cider vinegar

2 tablespoons Worcestershire sauce
2 tablespoons dry yellow mustard
2 tablespoon chili powder
2 teaspoons fresh ground black pepper
½ teaspoon ground ginger
¼ teaspoon fresh ground allspice
½ teaspoon cayenne pepper
¼ teaspoon ground mace
2½ tablespoons honey
2 cups tomato catsup

In a large saucepan, combine all sauce ingredients. Heat on medium, stirring will to mix and dissolve the spices. Reduce and simmer the sauce, uncovered for 30 minutes, stirring occasionally.

Ribs:
4 slabs of pork spareribs with tips attached

Remove the thick membrane covering the bone side of the slab. Separate the membrane at one end of the slab by slitting it with a knife and forcing your fingers underneath. Pull down the length of the slab and discard membrane. On the meaty side of slab, trim membrane on bottom of rib line. Using a sharp knife, remove rib tip, cutting parallel to bottom of slab. Cut rib tips into several pieces. Sprinkle the rub amply over both sides of ribs and tips. To barbecue: Start grill on low heat and allow to warm for 30 minutes. Fill bread loaf pan half-full of water and place on grill. Cook the ribs for 2 hours at about 230-250°F. After 2 hours turn ribs and grill for another 2 hours at same temperature. For glazing ribs: Put portion of sauce in a separate container and brush on both sides of ribs every 15 minutes during last half-hour of cooking time. Remove the ribs and set for 10 minutes. Cut into individual pieces, and serve with extra sauce. Experiment with combinations of the rub and sauce for individual preferences. ENJOY.

Host and Hostess: Boone and Alice Whitmer

Address and Contact Numbers:

872 Nickwall Road, Wolf Point,
MT 59201
1-406-525-3289

Location:

From Wolf Point travel south on
Highway 25 to Highway 13. Cross
bridge. Travel 2 miles south on
Highway 13 to mile marker 44 on

top of hill. Turn left on gravel road. Go 8.6 miles. Turn left to Meadowlark
driveway.

Hilltop House

The **Hilltop House Bed and Breakfast** in Westby borders North Dakota. As Susan and Ellis Hagen, the owners of Hilltop, say, "From our window we have the sunrise of North Dakota, the panorama of Canada and the sunset of Montana." Westby, in its early days, was in the "dry" state of North Dakota. Preferring Montana, the citizens of Westby moved their town, by rail, across the border to Montana.

The Hagen's many hobbies make life entertaining for their guests. Westby's agricultural setting produces beautiful flowers and herbs. Dried wreathes and bouquets are sold at Clara's Treasures, the gift shop at Hilltop House. Birders add new sightings to their list of flickers, warblers, hawks and game birds. Susan has a personal interest in the topic of "motherless daughters." She hosts workshops on topics related to counseling.

The Hilltop house is pert and pretty in stencils, houseplants, homemade quilts and country landscaping. Susan sponsors several local

artists and their work is displayed and sold at the Hilltop. The upstairs guest area is filled with family heirlooms and treasures. The rooms are called the Western Prairie Room and the Prairie Rose Room in honor of the landscape seen from the hilltop setting.

Rhubarb Coffee Cake

Topping:
½ cup granulated sugar
½ cup finely chopped walnuts
1 tablespoon melted butter
1 teaspoon cinnamon
Thoroughly combine dry ingredients, add
butter and set aside.

Dough:
1½ cups firmly packed brown sugar
½ cup margarine
1 egg
2 cups flour
1 teaspoon baking soda
½ teaspoon salt
1 cup sour cream
1½ cup finely diced rhubarb

Combine and sift dry ingredients, set aside. Combine sugar, margarine
and egg. Add dry to liquid ingredients alternately with sour cream.
Stir in rhubarb. Spread in 9x13-inch greased and floured baking pan.
Sprinkle with topping and bake for 35-40 minutes at 350°F, or when
center retains shape when touched. Cool for 20 minutes, cut, serve.

**Host and Hostess: Ellis and
Susan Hagen**
Address and Contact Numbers:
301 East 2nd Street, Westby, MT
59275
1-406-385-2508, 1-406-385-2533

Double J Montana

An aerial view of Glasgow, Montana shows it accessibility to the surrounding country-side. As you look at the roll-ing prairie beyond the town site, there is a bluff that rises above the Milk River. At the top of the prominence with a

three hundred and sixty degree view of the valley is the **Double J Montana Bed and Breakfast**. The Double J is on two hundred and sixty acres of wheat and hunting land. It is accessible by road and rail as Montana Highway 2 and Amtrak run below the hill about two miles from the main ranch site.

Jackie and John Stanislaw are the owners of the Double J. They came from New York and have expanded the outreach of one of Montana's long-standing newspapers, the *Glasgow Courier*. They were attracted to the open prairies and have made the ranch a hunting destination for bed and breakfast guests and friends and acquaintances beyond the borders of the Northwest.

The Double J, designed by Jackie, is built around an open staircase constructed of local tamarack timbers. Window space at three levels of this spacious home allow you views of the surrounding valley. The views reach above the thicket where deer graze and come to the river at dawn and dusk. A wrap around deck and swimming pool are extras to accommodate guests in the summer months.

The main house has three guestrooms each with a spe-cial feature. The tranquility of a favorite room for morning light is not outdone by the

room that faces the twinkling night lights of Glasgow. Yet another has its own skylight. The breakfast is a gourmet treat and finds either John or Jackie in the kitchen making the preparations for Fresh Strawberry Puff Pancake from the *Montana Cookbook*.

Fresh Strawberry Puff Pancake

¼ cup butter
3 eggs
1½ cups milk
6 tablespoon sugar
¾ cup flour
¼ teaspoon salt
3 cups strawberries, halved
sour cream
brown sugar

Place butter in a 9-inch springform pan. Place pan in a 425°F oven until butter melts and bubbles, about 2-5 minutes. Meanwhile, beat together eggs, milk, 4 tablespoons sugar, flour, and salt until smooth. Pour batter quickly into hot butter. Return to oven and bake 30 minutes or until edges are puffed and brown. Sprinkle strawberries with remaining sugar and stir to coat evenly. When pancake is done, remove from oven and spoon straw- berries into center. Cut into wedges and serve with sour cream and brown sugar. Serves four.

Host and Hostess: John and Jackie Stanislaw
Address and Contact Numbers:
Box 75, Vandalia, MT 59273
1-406-367-5353
Location:
13 miles west of Glasgow

Stage Road Inn

Very near Canada at the far reaches of the Highline or Highway 2 is the ranching area of Dodson. It prospered and made history with a gold strike in Zortman and the coming of the Great Northern Railroad of James J. Hill. Sandy Calk is the owner of the Dodson **Stageroad Inn Bed and Breakfast**. Sandy is a native Montanan who appreciates the life in this broad valley near the Fort Belnap Reservation.

The home which is now the Stage Road Inn once stood in Savoy. It was built for James J. Hill in 1905. Later the home was moved to the Stage Road site, where mule trains and stage coaches were the forerunners of the Iron Horse as it served the Zortman gold mining district fifty miles south of Dodson. Dodson was the hub on the Milk River which connected trade and traders to the wide Missouri

Sandy promotes the art and artistry of the Native Americans in the Dodson and Fort Belnap area. One important piece and person is Two-Gun White-Cat whose profile is on the Indian Head nickel. A more infamous varmint is on a most-wanted poster. Harvey Logan alias Kid Curry, robbed the train with its gold shipment from the Landusky Mine when Montana was still a territory. In that day, four thousand dollars

was a fortune to offer for his capture, dead or alive. He never came to public justice.

The Stage Road has expanded facilities with a private bath. Sandy offers this easy and economical recipe.

Refrigerator Muffins

2 cups shredded wheat cereal
4 cups all-bran cereal
2 cups boiling water
2 cups sugar
1 cup shortening
4 eggs, beaten
5 cups flour
5 teaspoons soda
½ teaspoon salt
4 cups buttermilk

Soak shredded wheat and all-bran in boiling water and set aside. Meanwhile, cream sugar and shortening, add eggs. Sift soda, flour, and salt. Add to liquid mixture. Add buttermilk. Combine with wheat and bran mixture. Mix well. Pour into gallon jug and store in refrigerator. Use as needed, filling greased or paper-lined muffin tins ¾ full. Bake at 375°F for 25 minutes or until rich brown. Makes one gallon and will keep refrigerated.

Hostess: Sandy Calk
Address and Contact Numbers:
Box 6, Dodson, MT 59524
1-406-383-4410

References

Badger, Lorraine. 1994. "Oven-Roasted Potatoes." *Complete Vegetable Cookbook*. New York, New York: Crown Publishers, Inc.

"Chuck and Apples." 1975. *Successful Farming*. Des Moines, Iowa: Meredith Corporation.

DeHaas, John N. 1963. *Montana's Historic Structures, Volume One*. Bozeman, Montana: Montana State University and the National Park Service.

Elwood, Henry. 1990. *Somers, Montana*. Kalispell, Montana: Thomas Printing, Inc.

Grant, Frank R., Lecture Series. 1986. "K. Ross Toole's Montana." Missoula, Montana: University of Montana.

Hachfeld, Linda and Eykyn, Betsy. 1992. *Cooking Á Lá Heart*. Mankato, Minnesota: Apple Tree Press.

Johnson, D. M. 1971. *The Bloody Bozeman: The Perilous Trail to Montana's Gold*. New York, New York: McGraw-Hill.

Johnstad, Ronald I. 1996. *Montana As I Remember It*. Eau Claire, Wisconsin: Heins Publications.

Krumm, Bob. 1991. *The Rocky Mountain Berry Book*. Helena, Montana: Falcon Press.

Leopold, Aldo. 1949. *A Sand County Almanac and Sketches Here and There*. New York, New York: Oxford University Press.

Lewis, Meriweather, and Clark, William, DeVoto, Bernard, Editor. 1953. *The Journals of Lewis and Clark*. New York, New York: Houghton Mifflin Company.

Lobsenz, Norman. 1959. *The First Book of National Monuments*. New York, New York: Franklin Watts, Inc.

Logan, Mike. 1990. *Laugh Kills Lonesome*. Helena, Montana: Buglin' Bull Press.

Maddex, Diane. 1985. *Built in the U. S. A.: American Buildings from Airports to Zoos*. Washington, D. C.: The Preservation Press.

McClun, Diana, and Nownes, Laura. 1993. *Quilts, Quilts, and More Quilts*. Layfayette, California: C and T Publishing.

McDonald, James R. 1984. *Bozeman's Historic Resources*. Bozeman, Montana: Bozeman Historic Resource Surveys.

McGinnis, Lilian. 1990. "Fresh Strawberry Puff Pancake." *The Montana Cookbook*. Edited by M. E. Holverson and G. C. Shirley. Helena, Montana: Falcon Press.

McGrath, Jean. 1976. *Butte Heritage Cookbook*. Butte, Montana: Silverbow Centennial Commission.

Myers, Rex C. and Fritz, Harry W., Editors. 1984. *Montana and the West: Essays in Honor of K. Ross Toole*. Boulder, Colorado: Pruett Publishing Company.

National Geographi.1999. *Birder's Journal*. Washington, D. C.

O'Neill, Molly. 1992. "Black and White Cookies." *New York Cookbook*. New York, New York: Workman Publishing Company. (Republished in *Choclatier*, 1995.)

"Pear Coffee Cake." January/February 1997. *Cooking Light*. Birmingham, Alabama.

Rifkind, Carole. 1980 *A Field Guide to American Architecture*. New York, New York: New American Library.

Riley, Glenda. 1996. *The Building and Breaking of Families in the American West*. Albuquerque, New Mexico: University of New Mexico Press.

Rodgers, D. 1967 *The House in My Head*. New York, New York: Atheneum.

Sanders, Wilbur Fisk. 1883. "Biscuits to Badmen." Butte, Montana: Editorial Review Press.

Scherger, R. H. 1996. "Charles Krug: High Society on the Frontier." Glendive, Montana: A Publishing House.

Sinclair, P. B. 1985. *Victorious Victorians*. New York, New York: Holt, Rinehart, and Winston.

Skees, Darlene Glantz. 1990. "Apple-Brandy French Toast with Cinnamon Syrup." *Best of Friends, Too Cookbook*. Helena, Montana: Two Dot Press.

Uecker, Bobbi. 1990. "French Toast with Sautéed Fruit." *The Montana Cookbook*. Edited by M. E. Holverson and G. C. Shirley. Helena, Montana: Falcon Press.

Wolle, Muriel Sibell. 1983. *Montana Pay Dirt: A Guide to the Mining Camps of the Treasure State*. Denver, Colorado: Sage Press.

USGS Topographic Map of Montana

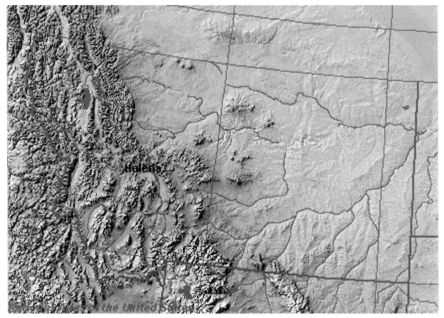

http://www.nationalatlas.gov

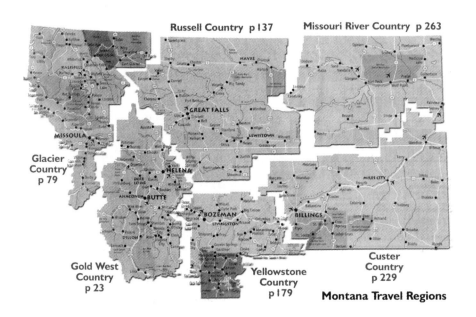

Russell Country p 137

Missouri River Country p 263

Glacier Country p 79

Gold West Country p 23

Yellowstone Country p 179

Custer Country p 229

Montana Travel Regions

Index

About the Author and the Photographer

Janet and Steve Colberg and Summer Kitchen Press proudly present the Second Edition of *Montana Bed and Breakfast Guide and Cookbook*. The Colbergs travel extensively and find joy in sharing their adventures. They have visited and photographed the United States, including Maine, Hawaii, Florida and Alaska. Their travels outside of the United States have taken them to Europe, Asia, the Caribbean, the Middle East, India, Canada and Mexico. Steve served as a high school math teacher and Janet was a director of a nursing school in the United States Peace Corps in Lashkar Gah, Afghanistan.

Steve is retired from work as a statistician and systems analyst for the State of Montana. He now owns an internet store featuring Montana products, www.BiggerSky.com, and a web/internet development business, www.WebByPros.com. Janet worked as a school nurse for the Helena School District and presently is a licensed professional counselor and operates Summer Kitchen Press. They are the parents of two grown sons, Jason and Joshua.

Janet and Steve hope this updated and expanded version about Montana's fine bed and breakfast homes will make your travels more enjoyable. Both the number of bed and breakfasts and the number of recipes are more than doubled in this edition. Notes on a few historical features, some outstanding recipes from the bed and breakfast owners together with hundreds of pictures from the homes and locations will delight any armchair traveler as well.

Travel Notes

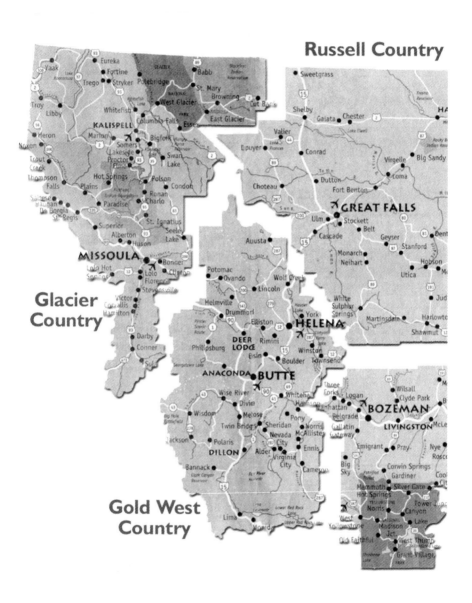

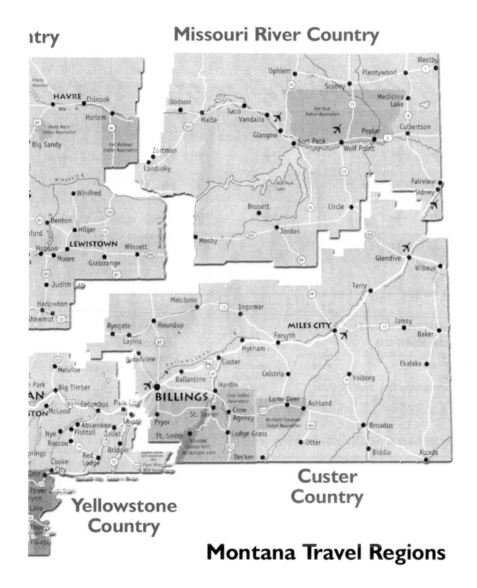

Missouri River Country

Montana Travel Regions

Yellowstone Country

Custer Country

Name
Address
Phone No.

Name
Address
Phone No.

Name
Address
Phone No.

Name
Address
Phone No.

Name
Address
Phone No.

Name
Address
Phone No.

Name
Address
Phone No.

Name
Address
Phone No.

Name
Address
Phone No.

Order Form

Summer Kitchen Press
314 Chaucer Street
Helena, MT 59601-5362
Web Address: http://www.BiggerSky.com/SKP

Date _____

Montana Bed and Breakfast Guide and Cookbook

Number of copies _____   @ US$14.95 $ _____
    Subtract any discount(s)   _____
    Add Shipping & Handling   @ $2.00/book   _____

_____ **TOTAL** $ _____

Ship to:
    Name _____
    Organization _____
    Address _____
    City, State, Zip _____
    Phone Number _____
    Email Address _____

Bill to (select payment method):
() Payment enclosed*
() Credit Card, Select: () Visa () MasterCard
    Name on card _____
    Bank _____
    Card Number _____
    Expiration Date (mm/yy)   _____/_____
() Purchase Order
    P.O. Number _____
    Name _____
    Organization _____
    Address _____
    City, State, Zip _____
() Prepaid: Date _____, Amount $ _____

*Make checks payable to Summer Kitchen Press.